Mental Mindset

Unleashing the Power Within

Swami Vivekananda

Institute of Thought & Philosophy

GRAPEVINE INDIA

Published by

GRAPEVINE INDIA PUBLISHERS PVT LTD

www.grapevineindia.com
Delhi | Mumbai
email: grapevineindiapublishers@gmail.com

Ordering Information:
Quantity sales: Special discounts are available on quantity purchases by corporations, associations, and others.
For details, reach out to the publisher.

First published by Grapevine India 2023

The mission of the Institute of Thought and Philosophy is to preserve and propagate the teachings of Swami Vivekananda. This great Indian spiritual leader is known for introducing the West to Hinduism. Drawing from his vast literary legacy, we provide valuable insights and practical guidance for modern living.

Have any query or feedback? Please reach out to us at ITPPress123@gmail.com

Developing Character

The road to the Good is the roughest and steepest in the universe. It is a wonder that so many succeed, no wonder that so many fall. Character has to be established through a thousand stumbles.

Wait, money does not pay, nor name; fame does not pay, nor learning. It is love that pays; it is character that cleaves its way through adamantine walls of difficulties.

Every work that we do, every movement of the body, every thought that we think, leaves such an impression on the mind-stuff, and even when such impressions are not obvious on the surface, they are sufficiently strong to work beneath the surface, subconsciously. What we are every moment is determined by the sum total of these impressions on the mind.

What I am just at this moment is the effect of the sum total of all the impressions of my past life. This is really what is meant by character; each man's character is determined by the sum total of these impressions.

If good impressions prevail, the character becomes good; if bad, it becomes bad. If a man continuously hears bad words, thinks bad thoughts, does bad actions, his mind will be full of bad impressions; and they will influence his thought and work without his being conscious of the fact.

In fact, these bad impressions are always working, and their resultant must be evil, and that man will be a bad man; he cannot help it. The sum total of these impressions in him will create the strong motive power for doing bad actions. He will be like a machine in the hands of his impressions, and they will force him to do evil.

Similarly, if a man thinks good thoughts and does good works, the sum total of these impressions will be good; and they, in a similar manner, will force him to do good even in spite of himself. When a man has done so much good work and thought so many good thoughts that there is an irresistible tendency in him to do good in spite of himself. Even if he wishes to do evil, his mind, as the sum total of his tendencies, will not allow him to do so; the tendencies will turn him back; he is completely under the influence of the good tendencies. When such is the case, a man's good character is said to be established.

As the tortoise tucks its feet and head inside the shell, and you may kill it and break it in pieces, and yet it will not come out, even so the character of that man who has control over his motives and organs is unchangeably established. He controls his own inner forces, and nothing can draw them out against his will.

By this continuous reflex of good thoughts, good impressions moving over the surface of the mind, the tendency for doing good becomes strong. And as the result we feel able to control the Indriyas (the sense-organs, the nerve-centres).

Thus alone will character be established, then alone a man gets to truth. Such a man is safe for ever; he cannot do any evil. You may place him in any company, there will be no danger for him.

There is a still higher state than having this good tendency, and that is the desire for liberation. You must remember that freedom of the soul is the goal of all Yogas, and each one equally leads to the same result.

By work alone men may get to where Buddha got largely by meditation or Christ by prayer. Buddha was a working Jnâni, Christ was a Bhakta, but the same goal was reached by both of them.

The difficulty is here. Liberation means entire freedom — freedom from the bondage of good, as well as from the bondage of evil. A golden chain is as much a chain as an iron one.

There is a thorn in my finger, and I use another to take the first one out; and when I have taken it out, I throw both of them aside; I have no necessity for keeping the second thorn, because both are thorns after all.

So the bad tendencies are to be counteracted by the good ones, and the bad impressions on the mind should be removed by the fresh waves of good ones, until all that is evil almost disappears, or is subdued and held in control in a corner of the mind; but after that, the good tendencies have also to be conquered.

Thus the "attached" becomes the "unattached". Work, but let not the action or the thought produce a deep impression on the mind. Let the ripples come and go, let huge actions proceed from the muscles and the brain, but let them not make any deep impression on the soul.

If you really want to judge of the character of a man, look not at his great performances. Every fool may become a hero at one time or another. Watch a man do his most common actions; those are indeed the things which will tell you the real character of a great man.

Great occasions rouse even the lowest of human beings to some kind of greatness, but he alone is the really great man whose character is great always, the same wherever he be.

Karma in its effect on character is the most tremendous power that man has to deal with. Man is, as it were, a centre, and is attracting all the powers of the universe towards himself, and in this centre is fusing them all and again sending them off in a big current.

Such a centre is the real man — the almighty, the omniscient — and he draws the whole universe towards him. Good and bad, misery and happiness, all are running towards him and clinging round him; and out of them he fashions the mighty stream of tendency called character and throws it outwards. As he has the power of drawing in anything, so has he the power of throwing it out.

The goal of mankind is knowledge. That is the one ideal placed before us by Eastern philosophy. Pleasure is not the goal of man, but knowledge. Pleasure and happiness come to an end.

It is a mistake to suppose that pleasure is the goal. The cause of all the miseries we have in the world is that men foolishly think pleasure to be the ideal to strive for.

After a time man finds that it is not happiness, but knowledge, towards which he is going, and that both pleasure and pain are great teachers, and that he learns as much from evil as from good. As pleasure and pain pass before his soul they have upon it different pictures, and the result of these combined impressions is what is called man's "character".

If you take the character of any man, it really is but the aggregate of tendencies, the sum total of the bent of his mind; you will find that misery and happiness are equal factors in the formation of that character. Good and evil have an equal share in moulding character, and in some instances, misery is a greater teacher than happiness.

In studying the great characters, the world has produced, I dare say, in the vast majority of cases, it would be found that it was misery that taught more than happiness, it was poverty that taught more than wealth, it was blows that brought out their inner fire more than praise.

What we call mistakes or evil, we commit because we are weak, and we are weak because we are ignorant. I prefer to call them mistakes. The word sin, although originally a very good word, has got a certain flavour about it that frightens me.

Who makes us ignorant? We ourselves. We put our hands over our eyes and weep that it is dark. Take the hands away and there is light; the light exists always for us, the self-effulgent nature of the human soul.

Do you not hear what your modern scientific men say? What is the cause of evolution? Desire. The animal wants to do something, but does not find the environment favourable, and therefore develops a new body.

Who develops it? The animal itself, its will. You have developed from the lowest amoeba. Continue to exercise your will and it will take you higher still. The will is almighty.

If it is almighty, you may say, why cannot I do everything? But you are thinking only of your little self. Look back on yourselves from the state of the amoeba to the human being; who made all that? Your own will.

Can you deny then that it is almighty? That which has made you come up so high can make you go higher still. What you want is character, strengthening of the will.

If I teach you that your nature is evil, that you should go home and sit in sackcloth and ashes and weep your lives out because you took certain false steps, it will not help you, but will weaken you all the more, and I shall be showing you the road to more evil than good. If this room is full of darkness for thousands of years and you come in and begin to weep and wail, "Oh the darkness", will the darkness vanish? Strike a match and light comes in a moment.

What good will it do you to think all your lives, "Oh, I have done evil, I have made many mistakes"? It requires no ghost to tell us that.

Bring in the light and the evil goes in a moment. Build up your character, and manifest your real nature, the Effulgent, the Resplendent, the Ever-Pure, and call It up in everyone that you see.

I wish that everyone of us had come to such a state that even in the vilest of human beings we could see the Real Self within, and instead of condemning them, say, "Rise thou effulgent one, rise thou who art always pure, rise thou birthless and deathless, rise almighty, and manifest thy true nature. These little manifestations do not befit thee."

This is the highest prayer that the Advaita teaches. This is the one prayer, to remember our true nature, the God who is always within us, thinking of it always as infinite, almighty, ever-good, ever-beneficent, selfless, bereft of all limitations.

And because that nature is selfless, it is strong and fearless; for only to selfishness comes fear. He who has nothing to desire for himself, whom does he fear, and what can frighten him? What fear has death for him? What fear has evil for him?

So if we are Advaitists, we must think from this moment that our old self is dead and gone. The old Mr., Mrs., and Miss So-and-so are gone, they were mere superstitions, and what remains is the ever-pure, the ever-strong, the almighty, the all-knowing — that alone remains for us, and then all fear vanishes from us.

Who can injure us, the omnipresent? All weakness has vanished from us, and our only work is to arouse this knowledge in our fellow beings. We see that they too are the same pure self, only they do not know it; we must teach them, we must help them to rouse up their infinite nature.

This is what I feel to be absolutely necessary all over the world. These doctrines are old, older than many mountains possibly. All truth is eternal. Truth is nobody's property; no race, no individual can lay any exclusive claim to it. Truth is the nature of all souls. Who can lay an, special claim to it?

But it has to be made practical, to be made simple (for the highest truths are always simple), so that it may penetrate every pore of human society, and become the property of the highest intellects and the commonest minds, of the man, woman, and child at the same time. All these ratiocinations of logic, all these bundles of metaphysics, all these theologies and ceremonies may have been good in their own time, but let us try to make things simpler and bring about the golden days when every man will be a worshipper, and the Reality in every man will be the object of worship.

The miseries of the world cannot be cured by physical help only. Until man's nature changes, these physical needs will always arise, and miseries will always be felt, and no amount of physical help will cure them completely. The only solution of this problem is to make mankind pure. Ignorance is the mother of all the evil and all the misery we see. Let men have light, let them be pure and spiritually strong and educated, then alone will misery cease in the world, not before. We may convert every house in the country into a charity asylum, we may fill the land with hospitals, but the misery of man will still continue to exist until man's character changes.

Great work requires great and persistent effort for a long time. Neither need we trouble ourselves if a few fail. It is in the nature of things that many should fall, that troubles should come, that tremendous difficulties should arise, that selfishness and all the other devils in the human heart should struggle hard when they are about to be driven out by the fire of spirituality.

The road to the Good is the roughest and steepest in the universe. It is a wonder that so many succeed, no wonder that so many fall. Character has to be established through a thousand stumbles.

The greatest religion is to be true to your own nature. Have faith in yourselves! If you do not exist, how can God exist, or anybody else? Wherever you are, it is this mind that perceives even the Infinite. I see God, therefore He exists. If I cannot think of God, He does not exist [for me]. This is the grand march of our human progress.

These [great souls] are signposts on the way. That is all they are. They say, "Onward, brothers!" We cling to them; we never want to move. We do not want to think; we want others to think for us. The messengers fulfil their mission. They ask to be up and doing. A hundred years later we cling to the message and go to sleep.

Talking about faith and belief and doctrine is easy, but it is so difficult to build character and to stem the tide of the senses.

We succumb. We become hypocrites.

Religion is not a doctrine, not a rule. It is a process. That is all. Doctrines and rules are all for exercise. By that exercise we get strong and at last break the bonds and become free. Doctrine is of no use except for gymnastics. Through exercise the soul becomes perfect. That exercise is stopped when you say, "I believe."

"Making pleasure and misery the same, making success and defeat the same, do thou stand up and fight. (Ibid. 38.)

This is the beginning of another peculiar doctrine of the Gita — the doctrine of non-attachment. That is to say, we have to bear the result of our own actions because we attach ourselves to them. ... "Only what is done as duty for duty's sake ... can scatter the bondage of Karma." (Ibid. 39.) There is no danger that you can overdo it. ... "If you do even a little of it, [this Yoga will save you from the terrible round of birth and death]. (Ibid. 40.)

The mind, to have non-attachment, must be clear, good, and rational. Why should we practice concentration? Because each action is like the pulsations quivering over the surface of the lake.

The vibration dies out, and what is left? The impressions. When a large number of these impressions are left on the mind, they coalesce and become a habit.

It is said, "Habit is second nature", it is first nature also, and the whole nature of man; everything that we are is the result of habit.

That gives us consolation, because, if it is only habit, we can make and unmake it at any time. The Samskaras are left by these vibrations passing out of our mind, each one of them leaving its result. Our character is the sum-total of these marks, and according as some particular wave prevails one takes that tone. If good prevails, one becomes good; if wickedness, one becomes wicked; if joyfulness, one becomes happy.

What Is Duty

The ordinary idea of duty everywhere is that every good man follows the dictates of his conscience. But what is it that makes an act a duty?

If a Christian finds a piece of beef before him and does not eat it to save his own life, or will not give it to save the life of another man, he is sure to feel that he has not done his duty. But if a Hindu dares to eat that piece of beef or to give it to another Hindu, he is equally sure to feel that he too has not done his duty; the Hindu's training and education make him feel that way.

In the last century there were notorious bands of robbers in India called thugs; they thought it their duty to kill any man they could and take away his money; the larger the number of men they killed, the better they thought they were.

Ordinarily if a man goes out into the street and shoots down another man, he is apt to feel sorry for it, thinking that he has done wrong. But if the very same man, as a soldier in his regiment, kills not one but twenty, he is certain to feel glad and think that he has done his duty remarkably well.

Therefore we see that it is not the thing done that defines a duty. To give an objective definition of duty is thus entirely impossible.

Yet there is duty from the subjective side. Any action that makes us go Godward is a good action, and is our duty; any action that makes us go downward is evil, and is not our duty.

From the subjective standpoint we may see that certain acts have a tendency to exalt and ennoble us, while certain other acts have a tendency to degrade and to brutalise us. But it is not possible to make out with certainty which acts have which kind of tendency in relation to all persons, of all sorts and conditions.

There is, however, only one idea of duty which has been universally accepted by all mankind, of all ages and sects and countries, and that has been summed up in a Sanskrit aphorism thus: "Do not injure any being; not injuring any being is virtue, injuring any being is sin."

The idea of duty varies much among different nations. In one country, if a man does not do certain things, people will say he has acted wrongly; while if he does those very things in another country, people will say that he did not act rightly — and yet we know that there must be some universal idea of duty. In the same way, one class of society thinks that certain things are among its duty, while another class thinks quite the opposite and would be horrified if it had to do those things.

Two ways are left open to us — the way of the ignorant, who think that there is only one way to truth and that all the rest are wrong, and the way of the wise, who admit that, according to our mental constitution or the different planes of existence in which we are, duty and morality may vary.

The important thing is to know that there are gradations of duty and of morality — that the duty of one state of life, in one set of circumstances, will not and cannot be that of another.

The Bhagavad-Gita frequently alludes to duties dependent upon birth and position in life. Birth and position in life and in society largely determine the mental and moral attitude of individuals towards the various activities of life. It is therefore our duty to do that work which will exalt and ennoble us in accordance with the ideals and activities of the society in which we are born.

But it must be particularly remembered that the same ideals and activities do not prevail in all societies and countries; our ignorance of this is the main cause of much of the hatred of one nation towards another. An American thinks that whatever an American does in accordance with the custom of his country is the best thing to do, and that whoever does not follow his custom must be a very wicked man. A Hindu thinks that his customs are the only right ones and are the best in the world, and that whosoever does not obey them must be the most wicked man living.

This is quite a natural mistake which all of us are apt to make. But it is very harmful; it is the cause of half the uncharitableness found in the world.

When I came to this country and was going through the Chicago Fair, a man from behind pulled at my turban. I looked back and saw that he was a very gentlemanly-looking man, neatly dressed. I spoke to him; and when he found that I knew English, he became very much abashed.

On another occasion in the same Fair another man gave me a push. When I asked him the reason, he also was ashamed and stammered out an apology saying, "Why do you dress that way?"

The sympathies of these men were limited within the range of their own language and their own fashion of dress. Much of the oppression of powerful nations on weaker ones is caused by this prejudice. It dries up their fellow feeling for fellow men.

That very man who asked me why I did not dress as he did and wanted to ill-treat me because of my dress may have been a very good man, a good father, and a good citizen; but the kindliness of his nature died out as soon as he saw a man in a different dress. Strangers are exploited in all countries, because they do not know how to defend themselves; thus they carry home false impressions of the peoples they have seen.

Sailors, soldiers, and traders behave in foreign lands in very queer ways, although they would not dream of doing so in their own country; perhaps this is why the Chinese call Europeans and Americans "foreign devils". They could not have done this if they had met the good, the kindly sides of Western life.

We should always try to see the duty of others through their own eyes, and never judge the customs of other peoples by our own standard. I am not the standard of the universe. I have to accommodate myself to the world, and not the world to me. So we see that environments change the nature of our duties, and doing the duty which is ours at any particular time is the best thing we can do in this world. Let us do that duty which is ours by birth; and when we have done that, let us do the duty which is ours by our position in life and in society.

There is, however, one great danger in human nature, viz that man never examines himself. He thinks he is quite as fit to be on the throne as the king. Even if he is, he must first show that he has done the duty of his own position; and then higher duties will come to him. When we begin to work earnestly in the world, nature gives us blows right and left and soon enables us to find out our position.

No man can long occupy satisfactorily a position for which he is not fit. There is no use in grumbling against nature's adjustment. He who does the lower work is not therefore a lower man. No man is to be judged by the mere nature of his duties, but all should be judged by the manner and the spirit in which they perform them.

Later on we shall find that even this idea of duty undergoes change, and that the greatest work is done only when there is no selfish motive to prompt it. Yet it is work through the sense of duty that leads us to work without any idea of duty; when work will become worship — nay, something higher — then will work be done for its own sake.

We shall find that the philosophy of duty, whether it be in the form of ethics or of love, is the same as in every other Yoga — the object being the attenuating of the lower self, so that the real higher Self may shine forth — the lessening of the frittering away of energies on the lower plane of existence, so that the soul may manifest itself on the higher ones. This is accomplished by the continuous denial of low desires, which duty rigorously requires.

The whole organisation of society has thus been developed, consciously or unconsciously, in the realms of action and experience, where, by limiting selfishness, we open the way to an unlimited expansion of the real nature of man.

Devotion To Duty

Each duty has its own place, and according to the circumstances in which we are placed, we must perform our duties. what is duty for one is not duty for another. At the same time, we do not say that this duty is lowering and the other elevating.

Isolation of the soul from all objects, mental and physical, is the goal; when that is attained, the soul will find that it was alone all the time, and it required no one to make it happy. As long as we require someone else to make us happy, we are slaves. When the Purusha finds that It is free, and does not require anything to complete Itself, that this nature is quite unnecessary, then freedom (Kaivalya) is attained.

Men run after a few dollars and do not think anything of cheating a fellow-being to get those dollars; but if they would restrain themselves, in a few years they would develop such characters as would bring them millions of dollars — if they wanted them. Then their will would govern the universe. But we are all such fools!

What is the use of talking of one's mistakes to the world? They cannot thereby be undone. For what one has done one must suffer; one must try and do better. The world sympathises only with the strong and the powerful.

It is only work that is done as a free-will offering to humanity and to nature that does not bring with it any binding attachment.

Duty of any kind is not to be slighted. A man who does the lower work is not, for that reason only, a lower man than he who does the higher work; a man should not be judged by the nature of his duties, but by the manner in which he does them. His manner of doing them and his power to do them are indeed the test of a man. A shoemaker who can turn out a strong, nice pair of shoes in the shortest possible time is a better man, according to his profession and his work, than a professor who talks nonsense every day of his life.

Every duty is holy, and devotion to duty is the highest form of the worship of God; it is certainly a source of great help in enlightening and emancipating the deluded and ignorance-encumbered souls of the Baddhas — the bound ones.

By doing well the duty which is nearest to us, the duty which is in our hands now, we make ourselves stronger and improving our strength in this manner step by step, we may even reach a state in which it shall be our privilege to do the most coveted and honoured duties in life and in society.

Our first duty is not to hate ourselves, because to advance we must have faith in ourselves first and then in God. He who has no faith in himself can never have faith in God. Therefore, the only alternative remaining to us is to recognise that duty and morality vary under different circumstances; not that the man who resists evil is doing what is always and in itself wrong, but that in the different circumstances in which he is placed it may become even his duty to resist evil.

All great teachers have taught, "Resist not evil," that non-resistance is the highest moral ideal. We all know that, if a certain number of us attempted to put that maxim fully into practice, the whole social fabric would fall to pieces, the wicked would take possession of our properties and our lives, and would do whatever they liked with us. Even if only one day of such non-resistance were practiced, it would lead to disaster.

Yet, intuitively, in our heart of hearts we feel the truth of the teaching "Resist not evil." This seems to us to be the highest ideal; yet to teach this doctrine only would be equivalent to condemning a vast portion of mankind.

Not only so, it would be making men feel that they were always doing wrong, and cause in them scruples of conscience in all their actions; it would weaken them, and that constant self-disapproval would breed more vice than any other weakness would. To the man who has begun to hate himself the gate to degeneration has already opened; and the same is true of a nation.

He who has no faith in himself can never have faith in God. Therefore, the only alternative remaining to us is to recognise that duty and morality vary under different circumstances; not that the man who resists evil is doing what is always and in itself wrong, but that in the different circumstances in which he is placed it may become even his duty to resist evil.

You should cultivate a noble nature by doing your duty. By doing our duty we get rid of the idea of duty; and then and then only we feel everything as done by God. We are but machines in His hand. This body is opaque, God is the lamp. Whatever is going out of the body is God's.

You do not feel it. You feel "I". This is delusion. You must learn calm submission to the will of God. Duty is the best school for it. This duty is morality.

Drill yourself to be thoroughly submissive. Get rid of the "I". No humbuggism. Then you can get rid of the idea of duty; for all is His. Then you go on naturally, forgiving, forgetting, etc.

Our religion always presents different gradations of duty and religion to different people.

Duty is seldom sweet. It is only when love greases its wheels that it runs smoothly; it is a continuous friction otherwise.

How else could parents do their duties to their children, husbands to their wives, and vice versa? Do we not meet with cases of friction every day in our lives? Duty is sweet only through love, and love shines in freedom alone.

Yet is it freedom to be a slave to the senses, to anger, to jealousies and a hundred other petty things that must occur every day in human life? In all these little roughnesses that we meet with in life, the highest expression of freedom is to forbear.

Women, slaves to their own irritable, jealous tempers, are apt to blame their husbands, and assert their own "freedom", as they think, not knowing that thereby they only prove that they are slaves. So it is with husbands who eternally find fault with their wives.

There is a sage in India, a great Yogi, one of the most wonderful men I have ever seen in my life. He is a peculiar man, he will not teach any one; if you ask him a question he will not answer. It is too much for him to take up the position of a teacher, he will not do it. If you ask a question, and wait for some days, in the course of conversation he will bring up the subject, and wonderful light will he throw on it.

He told me once the secret of work, "Let the end and the means be joined into one." When you are doing any work, do not think of anything beyond. Do it as worship, as the highest worship, and devote your whole life to it for the time being.

Thus, in the story, the Vyadha and the woman did their duty with cheerfulness and whole-heartedness; and the result was that they became illuminated, clearly showing that the right performance of the duties of any station in life, without attachment to results, leads us to the highest realisation of the perfection of the soul.

It is the worker who is attached to results that grumbles about the nature of the duty which has fallen to his lot. To the unattached worker all duties are equally good, and form efficient instruments with which selfishness and sensuality may be killed, and the freedom of the soul secured.

We are all apt to think too highly of ourselves. Our duties are determined by our desires to a much larger extent than we are willing to grant. Competition rouses envy, and it kills the kindliness of the heart. To the grumbler all duties are distasteful; nothing will ever satisfy him, and his whole life is doomed to prove a failure.

Let us work on, doing as we go whatever happens to be our duty, and being ever ready to put our shoulders to the wheel. Then surely shall we see the Light!

Karma-Yoga teaches us that the ordinary idea of duty is on the lower plane; nevertheless, all of us have to do our duty. Yet we may see that this peculiar sense of duty is very often a great cause of misery.

Duty becomes a disease with us; it drags us ever forward. It catches hold of us and makes our whole life miserable. It is the bane of human life. This duty, this idea of duty is the midday summer sun which scorches the innermost soul of mankind.

Look at those poor slaves to duty! Duty leaves them no time to say prayers, no time to bathe. Duty is ever on them. They go out and work. Duty is on them!

They come home and think of the work for the next day. Duty is on them! It is living a slave's life, at last dropping down in the street and dying in harness, like a horse.

This is duty as it is understood.

What is duty after all? It is really the impulsion of the flesh, of our attachment; and when an attachment has become established, we call it duty. It is, so to say, a sort of chronic disease. When it is acute, we call it disease; when it is chronic, we call it nature. It is a disease.

So when attachment becomes chronic, we baptise it with the high sounding name of duty. We strew flowers upon it, trumpets sound for it, sacred texts are said over it, and then the whole world fights, and men earnestly rob each other for this duty's sake.

Duty is good to the extent that it checks brutality. To the lowest kinds of men, who cannot have any other ideal, it is of some good; but those who want to be Karma-Yogis must throw this idea of duty overboard. There is no duty for you and me. Whatever you have to give to the world, do give by all means, but not as a duty. Do not take any thought of that. Be not compelled.

Unity in variety is the plan of creation. However men and women may vary individually, there is unity in the background. The different individual characters and classes of men and women are natural variations in creation.

Hence, we ought not to judge them by the same standard or put the same ideal before them. Such a course creates only an unnatural struggle, and the result is that man begins to hate himself and is hindered from becoming religious and good. Our duty is to encourage every one in his struggle to live up to his own highest ideal, and strive at the same time to make the ideal as near as possible to the truth.

In the material physical world, expansion is life, and contraction is death. Whatever ceases to expand ceases to live. Translating this in the moral world we have: If one would expand, he must love, and when he ceases to love he dies. It is your nature; you must, because that is the only law of life.

Therefore, we must love God for love's sake, so we must do our duty for duty's sake; we must work for work's sake without looking for any reward — know that you are purer and more perfect, know that this is the real temple of God.

Every man should take up his own ideal and endeavour to accomplish it. That is a surer way of progress than taking up other men's ideals, which he can never hope to accomplish.

For instance, we take a child and at once give him the task of walking twenty miles. Either the little one dies, or one in a thousand crawls the twenty miles, to reach the end exhausted and half-dead.

That is like what we generally try to do with the world. All the men and women, in any society, are not of the same mind, capacity, or of the same power to do things; they must have different ideals, and we have no right to sneer at any ideal. Let everyone do the best he can for realising his own ideal.

Nor is it right that I should be judged by your standard or you by mine. The apple tree should not be judged by the standard of the oak, nor the oak by that of the apple. To judge the apple tree you must take the apple standard, and for the oak, its own standard.

How Attachments are Formed

How can this be done? We see that the impression of any action, to which we attach ourselves, remains.

I may meet hundreds of persons during the day, and among them meet also one whom I love; and when I retire at night, I may try to think of all the faces I saw, but only that face comes before the mind — the face which I met perhaps only for one minute, and which I loved; all the others have vanished. My attachment to this particular person caused a deeper impression on my mind than all the other faces.

Physiologically the impressions have all been the same; every one of the faces that I saw pictured itself on the retina, and the brain took the pictures in, and yet there was no similarity of effect upon the mind. Most of the faces, perhaps, were entirely new faces, about which I had never thought before, but that one face of which I got only a glimpse found associations inside. Perhaps I had pictured him in my mind for years, knew hundreds of things about him, and this one new vision of him awakened hundreds of sleeping memories in my mind; and this one impression having been repeated perhaps a hundred times more than those of the different faces together, will produce a great effect on the mind.

Therefore, be "unattached"; let things work; let brain centres work; work incessantly, but let not a ripple conquer the mind. Work as if you were a stranger in this land, a sojourner; work incessantly, but do not bind yourselves; bondage is terrible. This world is not our habitation, it is only one of the many stages through which we are passing.

Remember that great saying of the Sânkhya, "The whole of nature is for the soul, not the soul for nature." The very reason of nature's existence is for the education of the soul; it has no other meaning; it is there because the soul must have knowledge, and through knowledge free itself.

If we remember this always, we shall never be attached to nature; we shall know that nature is a book in which we are to read, and that when we have gained the required knowledge, the book is of no more value to us.

Instead of that, however, we are identifying ourselves with nature; we are thinking that the soul is for nature, that the spirit is for the flesh, and, as the common saying has it, we think that man "lives to eat" and not "eats to live". We are continually making this mistake; we are regarding nature as ourselves and are becoming attached to it; and as soon as this attachment comes, there is the deep impression on the soul, which binds us down and makes us work not from freedom but like slaves.

Learn to help without pitying or feeling that there is any misery. Learn to be the same to enemy and to friend; then when you can do that and no longer have any desire, the goal is attained.

Cut down the banyan tree of desire with the axe of non-attachment, and it will vanish utterly. It is all illusion. "He from whom blight and delusion have fallen, he who has conquered the evils of association, he alone is âzâd (free)."

To love anyone personally is bondage. Love all alike, then all desires fall off.

Time, the "eater of everything", comes, and all has to go. Why try to improve the earth, to paint the butterfly? It all has to go at last. Do not be mere white mice in a treadmill, working always and never accomplishing anything. Every desire is fraught with evil, whether the desire itself be good or evil. It is like a dog jumping for a piece of meat which is ever receding from his reach, and dying a dog's death at last. Do not be like that. Cut off all desire.

By thinking about sense objects, attachment to them is formed. From attachment comes longing, and longing breeds anger.

From anger comes delusion, and from delusion, confused memory. From confused memory comes the ruin of discrimination; and from the ruin of discrimination, a man perishes.

There is then no peace in the heart of a carnal man, nor in him that is addicted to outward things, but in the spiritual and devout man.

The Vedanta philosophy says that this whole universe — mental, physical, moral — is hypnotic. Who is the cause of this hypnotism? You yourself are to blame. This weeping and wailing and knocking your heads into corners against brick walls, as it were will not do you the least good.

However, knocking everything [that is hypnotic] on the head [leads to] what is called non-attachment; and clinging to more and more hypnotism is attachment. That is why in all religions you will find they wanted to give up the world, although many of them do not understand it.

There was a poor man who wanted some money; and somehow, he had heard that if he could get hold of a ghost, he might command him to bring money or anything else he liked; so he was very anxious to get hold of a ghost. At last he found a sage with great powers, and besought his help. The sage asked him what he would do with a ghost.

"I want a ghost to work for me; teach me how to get hold of one, sir; I desire it very much," replied the man.

But the sage said, "Don't disturb yourself, go home."

The next day the man went again to the sage and began to weep and pray, "Give me a ghost; I must have a ghost, sir, to help me."

At last the sage was disgusted, and said, “Take this charm, repeat this magic word, and a ghost will come, and whatever you say to him he will do. But beware; they are terrible beings, and must be kept continually busy. If you fail to give him work, he will take your life.”

The man replied, “That is easy; I can give him work for all his life.”

Then he went to a forest, and after long repetition of the magic word, a huge ghost appeared before him, and said, “I am a ghost. I have been conquered by your magic; but you must keep me constantly employed. The moment you fail to give me work I will kill you.”

The man said, “Build me a palace,” and the ghost said, “It is done; the palace is built.” “

Bring me money,” said the man. “Here is your money,” said the ghost.

“Cut this forest down, and build a city in its place.”

“That is done,” said the ghost, “anything more?”

Now the man began to be frightened and thought he could give him nothing more to do; he did everything in a trice.

The ghost said, “Give me something to do or I will eat you up.”

The poor man could find no further occupation for him, and was frightened. So he ran and ran and at last reached the sage, and said, "Oh, sir, protect my life!"

The sage said, "I will find you a way out. Look at that dog with a curly tail. Draw your sword quickly and cut the tail off and give it to the ghost to straighten out."

The man cut off the dog's tail and gave it to the ghost, saying, "Straighten that out for me."

The ghost took it and slowly and carefully straightened it out, but as soon as he let it go, it instantly curled up again. Once more he laboriously straightened it out, only to find it again curled up as soon as he attempted to let go of it. Again he patiently straightened it out, but as soon as he let it go, it curled up again.

So he went on for days and days, until he was exhausted and said, "I was never in such trouble before in my life. I am an old veteran ghost, but never before was I in such trouble. I will make a compromise with you," he said to the man, "you let me off and I will let you keep all I have given you and will promise not to harm you."

The man was much pleased, and accepted the offer gladly.

This world is like a dog's curly tail, and people have been striving to straighten it out for hundreds of years; but when they let it go, it has curled up again. How could it be otherwise? One must first know how to work without attachment, then one will not be a fanatic.

When we know that this world is like a dog's curly tail and will never get straightened, we shall not become fanatics. If there were no fanaticism in the world, it would make much more progress than it does now.

It is a mistake to think that fanaticism can make for the progress of mankind. On the contrary, it is a retarding element creating hatred and anger, and causing people to fight each other, and making them unsympathetic. We think that whatever we do or possess is the best in the world, and what we do not do or possess is of no value.

So, always remember the instance of the curly tail of the dog whenever you have a tendency to become a fanatic. You need not worry or make yourself sleepless about the world; it will go on without you.

When you have avoided fanaticism, then alone will you work well. It is the level-headed man, the calm man, of good judgment and cool nerves, of great sympathy and love, who does good work and so does good to himself. The fanatic is foolish and has no sympathy; he can never straighten the world, nor himself become pure and perfect.

Let us work without desire for name or fame or rule over others. Let us be free from the triple bonds of lust, greed of gain, and anger. And this truth is with us!

Was Krishna cunning? No, he was not cunning. He tried his best to prevent the war. It was Duryodhana who forced the war. But, when once in the thing, you should not recede — that is the man of duty. Do not run away, it is cowardice. When in the thing, you must do it. You should not budge an inch — of course not for a wrong thing; this war was a righteous war.

The devil comes in many guises — anger in the form of justice — passion in the form of duty. When it first comes, the man knows and then he forgets. Just as your pleaders' conscience; at first they know it is all Badmâshi (roguery), then it is duty to their clients; at last they get hardened.

Leave off your commercial calculating ideas. If you can get rid of your attachment to a single thing, you are on the way to liberation.

Look at Krishna: he was great as a son, as a king, as a father, and all through his life he practiced the marvellous teachings which he preached." "He who in the midst of the greatest activity finds the sweetest peace, and in the midst of the greatest calmness is most active, he has known the secret of life."

Krishna shows the way how to do this — by being non-attached: do everything but do not get identified with anything. You are the soul, the pure, the free, all the time; you are the Witness. Our misery comes, not from work, but by our getting attached to something.

Take for instance, money: money is a great thing to have, earn it, says Krishna; struggle hard to get money, but don't get attached to it. So with children, with wife, husband, relatives, fame, everything; you have no need to shun them, only don't get attached.

There is only one attachment and that belongs to the Lord, and to none other. Work for them, love them, do good to them, sacrifice a hundred lives, if need be, for them, but never be attached. His own life was the exact exemplification of that.

Work and Unattachment

This whole universe is only one speck of the infinite being; and all our laws, our bondages, our joys and our sorrows, our happinesses and our expectations, are only within this small universe; all our progression and digression are within its small compass.

So you see how childish it is to expect a continuation of this universe — the creation of our minds — and to expect to go to heaven, which after all must mean only a repetition of this world that we know. You see at once that it is an impossible and childish desire to make the whole of infinite existence conform to the limited and conditioned existence which we know.

When a man says that he will have again and again this same thing which he is hating now, or, as I sometimes put it, when he asks for a comfortable religion, you may know that he has become so degenerate that he cannot think of anything higher than what he is now; he is just his little present surroundings and nothing more. He has forgotten his infinite nature, and his whole idea is confined to these little joys, and sorrows, and heart-jealousies of the moment.

He thinks that this finite thing is the infinite; and not only so, he will not let this foolishness go. He clings on desperately unto Trishnâ, and the thirst after life, what the Buddhists call Tanhâ and Tissâ. There may be millions of kinds of happiness, and beings, and laws, and progress, and causation, all acting outside the little universe that we know; and, after all, the whole of this comprises but one section of our infinite nature.

To acquire freedom we have to get beyond the limitations of this universe; it cannot be found here. Perfect equilibrium, or what the Christians call the peace that passeth all understanding, cannot be had in this universe, nor in heaven, nor in any place where our mind and thoughts can go, where the senses can feel, or which the imagination can conceive.

No such place can give us that freedom, because all such places would be within our universe, and it is limited by space, time, and causation. There may be places that are more ethereal than this earth of ours, where enjoyments may be keener, but even those places must be in the universe and, therefore, in bondage to law; so we have to go beyond, and real religion begins where this little universe ends. These little joys, and sorrows, and knowledge of things end there, and the reality begins.

Until we give up the thirst after life, the strong attachment to this our transient conditioned existence we have no hope of catching even a glimpse of that infinite freedom beyond. It stands to reason then that there is only one way to attain to that freedom which is the goal of all the noblest aspirations of mankind, and that is by giving up this little life, giving up this little universe, giving up this earth, giving up heaven, giving up the body, giving up the mind, giving up everything that is limited and conditioned.

If we give up our attachment to this little universe of the senses or of the mind, we shall be free immediately. The only way to come out of bondage is to go beyond the limitations of law, to go beyond causation.

But it is a most difficult thing to give up the clinging to this universe; few ever attain to that. There are two ways to do that mentioned in our books. One is called the "Neti, Neti" (not this, not this), the other is called "Iti" (this); the former is the negative, and the latter is the positive way.

The negative way is the most difficult. It is only possible to the men of the very highest, exceptional minds and gigantic wills who simply stand up and say, "No, I will not have this," and the mind and body obey their will, and they come out successful.

But such people are very rare. The vast majority of mankind choose the positive way, the way through the world, making use of all the bondages themselves to break those very bondages. This is also a kind of giving up; only it is done slowly and gradually, by knowing things, enjoying things and thus obtaining experience, and knowing the nature of things until the mind lets them all go at last and becomes unattached.

The former way of obtaining non-attachment is by reasoning, and the latter way is through work and experience. The first is the path of Jnâna-Yoga, and is characterized by the refusal to do any work; the second is that of Karma-Yoga, in which there is no cessation from work.

Every one must work in the universe. Only those who are perfectly satisfied with the Self, whose desires do not go beyond the Self, whose mind never strays out of the Self, to whom the Self is all in all, only those do not work. The rest must work.

A current rushing down of its own nature falls into a hollow and makes a whirlpool, and, after running a little in that whirlpool, it emerges again in the form of the free current to go on unchecked. Each human life is like that current. It gets into the whirl, gets involved in this world of space, time, and causation, whirls round a little, crying out, "my father, my brother, my name, my fame", and so on, and at last emerges out of it and regains its original freedom.

The whole universe is doing that. Whether we know it or not, whether we are conscious or unconscious of it, we are all working to get out of the dream of the world. Man's experience in the world is to enable him to get out of its whirlpool.

As children we all think that the world is made so very nice, and that masses of pleasures are simply waiting for our going out to them. That is every schoolboy's dream. And when he goes out into the world, the everyday world, very soon his dreams vanish. So with nations. When they see how every city is built upon ruins — every forest stands upon a city — then they become convinced of the vanity of this world.

All the power of knowledge and wealth once made has passed away — all the sciences of the ancients, lost, lost forever. Nobody knows how. That teaches us a grand lesson. Vanity of vanities; all is vanity and vexation of the spirit. If we have seen all this, then we become disgusted with this world and all it offers us. This is called Vairâgya, non-attachment, and is the first step towards knowledge.

To attain this unattachment is almost a life-work, but as soon as we have reached this point, we have attained the goal of love and become free; the bondage of nature falls from us, and we see nature as she is; she forges no more chains for us; we stand entirely free and take not the results of work into consideration; who then cares for what the results may be?

Do you ask anything from your children in return for what you have given them? It is your duty to work for them, and there the matter ends. In whatever you do for a particular person, a city, or a state, assume the same attitude towards it as you have towards your children — expect nothing in return. If you can invariably take the position of a giver, in which everything given by you is a free offering to the world, without any thought of return, then will your work bring you no attachment. Attachment comes only where we expect a return.

If working like slaves results in selfishness and attachment, working as master of our own mind gives rise to the bliss of non-attachment.

We say that we cannot do good without at the same time doing some evil, or do evil without doing some good.

Knowing this, how can we work? There have, therefore, been sects in this world who have in an astoundingly preposterous way preached slow suicide as the only means to get out of the world, because if a man lives, he has to kill poor little animals and plants or do injury to something or some one. So according to them the only way out of the world is to die.

The Jains have preached this doctrine as their highest ideal. This teaching seems to be very logical. But the true solution is found in the Gita. It is the theory of non-attachment, to be attached to nothing while doing our work of life.

Know that you are separated entirely from the world, though you are in the world, and that whatever you may be doing in it, you are not doing that for your own sake. Any action that you do for yourself will bring its effect to bear upon you. If it is a good action, you will have to take the good effect, and if bad, you will have to take the bad effect; but any action that is not done for your own sake, whatever it be, will have no effect on you.

There is to be found a very expressive sentence in our scriptures embodying this idea: "Even if he kill the whole universe (or be himself killed), he is neither the killer nor the killed, when he knows that he is not acting for himself at all."

Therefore Karma-Yoga teaches, "Do not give up the world; live in the world, imbibe its influences as much as you can; but if it be for your own enjoyment's sake, work not at all."

Enjoyment should not be the goal. First kill your self and then take the whole world as yourself; as the old Christians used to say, "The old man must die." This old man is the selfish idea that the whole world is made for our enjoyment.

Foolish parents teach their children to pray, "O Lord, Thou hast created this sun for me and this moon for me," as if the Lord has had nothing else to do than to create everything for these babies.

Do not teach your children such nonsense. Then again, there are people who are foolish in another way: they teach us that all these animals were created for us to kill and eat, and that this universe is for the enjoyment of men. That is all foolishness.

A tiger may say, "Man was created for me," and pray, "O Lord, how wicked are these men who do not come and place themselves before me to be eaten; they are breaking Your law."

If the world is created for us, we are also created for the world. That this world is created for our enjoyment is the most wicked idea that holds us down. This world is not for our sake. Millions pass out of it every year; the world does not feel it; millions of others are supplied in their place. Just as much as the world is for us, so we also are for the world.

To work properly, therefore, you have first to give up the idea of attachment. Secondly, do not mix in the fray, hold yourself as a witness and go on working.

My master used to say, "Look upon your children as a nurse does." The nurse will take your baby and fondle it and play with it and behave towards it as gently as if it were her own child; but as soon as you give her notice to quit, she is ready to start off bag and baggage from the house. Everything in the shape of attachment is forgotten; it will not give the ordinary nurse the least pang to leave your children and take up other children.

Even so are you to be with all that you consider your own. You are the nurse, and if you believe in God, believe that all these things which you consider yours are really His. The greatest weakness often insinuates itself as the greatest good and strength. It is a weakness to think that any one is dependent on me, and that I can do good to another. This belief is the mother of all our attachment, and through this attachment comes all our pain.

We must inform our minds that no one in this universe depends upon us; not one beggar depends on our charity; not one soul on our kindness; not one living thing on our help. All are helped on by nature, and will be so helped even though millions of us were not here. The course of nature will not stop for such as you and me; it is, as already pointed out, only a blessed privilege to you and to me that we are allowed, in the way of helping others, to educate ourselves.

This is a great lesson to learn in life, and when we have learned it fully, we shall never be unhappy; we can go and mix without harm in society anywhere and everywhere. You may have wives and husbands, and regiments of servants, and kingdoms to govern; if only you act on the principle that the world is not for you and does not inevitably need you, they can do you no harm.

This very year some of your friends may have died. Is the world waiting without going on, for them to come again? Is its current stopped? No, it goes on. So drive out of your mind the idea that you have to do something for the world; the world does not require any help from you.

It is sheer nonsense on the part of any man to think that he is born to help the world; it is simply pride, it is selfishness insinuating itself in the form of virtue. When you have trained your mind and your nerves to realise this idea of the world's non-dependence on you or on anybody, there will then be no reaction in the form of pain resulting from work.

When you give something to a man and expect nothing — do not even expect the man to be grateful — his ingratitude will not tell upon you, because you never expected anything, never thought you had any right to anything in the way of a return. You gave him what he deserved; his own Karma got it for him; your Karma made you the carrier thereof.

Why should you be proud of having given away something? You are the porter that carried the money or other kind of gift, and the world deserved it by its own Karma. Where is then the reason for pride in you? There is nothing very great in what you give to the world.

When you have acquired the feeling of non-attachment, there will then be neither good nor evil for you. It is only selfishness that causes the difference between good and evil. It is a very hard thing to understand, but you will come to learn in time that nothing in the universe has power over you until you allow it to exercise such a power. Nothing has power over the Self of man, until the Self becomes a fool and loses independence.

So, by non-attachment, you overcome and deny the power of anything to act upon you. It is very easy to say that nothing has the right to act upon you until you allow it to do so; but what is the true sign of the man who really does not allow anything to work upon him, who is neither happy nor unhappy when acted upon by the external world? The sign is that good or ill fortune causes no change in his mind: in all conditions he continues to remain the same.

In Krishna we find ... two ideas [stand] supreme in his message: The first is the harmony of different ideas; the second is non-attachment. A man can attain to perfection, the highest goal, sitting on a throne, commanding armies, working out big plans for nations. In fact, Krishna's great sermon was preached on the battlefield.

Krishna saw plainly through the vanity of all the mummeries, mockeries, and ceremonials of the old priests; and yet he saw some good in them.

This was the great work of Krishna: to clear our eyes and make us look with broader vision upon humanity in its march upward and onward. His was the first heart that was large enough to see truth in all, his the first lips that uttered beautiful words for each and all.

This Krishna preceded Buddha by some thousand years. ... A great many people do not believe that he ever existed. Some believe that [the worship of Krishna grew out of] the old sun worship. There seem to be several Krishnas: one was mentioned in the Upanishads, another was king, another a general. All have been lumped into one Krishna.

It does not matter much. The fact is, some individual comes who is unique in spirituality. Then all sorts of legends are invented around him. But, all the Bibles and stories which come to be cast upon this one person have to be recast in [the mould of] his character. All the stories of the New Testament have to be modelled upon the accepted life [and] character of Christ. In all of the Indian stories about Buddha the one central note of that whole life is kept up — sacrifice for others.

No one can get anything unless he earns it. This is an eternal law. We may sometimes think it is not so, but in the long run we become convinced of it. A man may struggle all his life for riches; he may cheat thousands, but he finds at last that he did not deserve to become rich, and his life becomes a trouble and a nuisance to him.

We may go on accumulating things for our physical enjoyment, but only what we earn is really ours. A fool may buy all the books in the world, and they will be in his library; but he will be able to read only those that he deserves to; and this deserving is produced by Karma.

Our Karma determines what we deserve and what we can assimilate. We are responsible for what we are; and whatever we wish ourselves to be, we have the power to make ourselves. If what we are now has been the result of our own past actions, it certainly follows that whatever we wish to be in future can be produced by our present actions; so we have to know how to act.

Karma-Yoga explains this secret and teaches where and how to work, how to employ to the greatest advantage the largest part of our energies in the work that is before us. But with this secret we must take into consideration the great objection against work, namely that it causes pain.

All misery and pain come from attachment. I want to do work; I want to do good to a human being; and it is ninety to one that that human being whom I have helped will prove ungrateful and go against me; and the result to me is pain. Such things deter mankind from working; and it spoils a good portion of the work and energy of mankind, this fear of pain and misery.

Karma-Yoga teaches us how to work for work's sake, unattached, without caring who is helped, and what for. The Karma-Yogi works because it is his nature, because he feels that it is good for him to do so, and he has no object beyond that.

His position in this world is that of a giver, and he never cares to receive anything. He knows that he is giving, and does not ask for anything in return and, therefore, he eludes the grasp of misery. The grasp of pain, whenever it comes, is the result of the reaction of "attachment".

I have been asked many times how we can work if we do not have the passion which we generally feel for work. I also thought in that way years ago, but as I am growing older, getting more experience, I find it is not true. The less passion there is, the better we work. The calmer we are, the better for us, and the more the amount of work we can do.

When we let loose our feelings, we waste so much energy, shatter our nerves, disturb our minds, and accomplish very little work. The energy which ought to have gone out as work is spent as mere feeling, which counts for nothing. It is only when the mind is very calm and collected that the whole of its energy is spent in doing good work.

And if you read the lives of the great workers which the world has produced, you will find that they were wonderfully calm men. Nothing, as it were, could throw them off their balance.

That is why the man who becomes angry never does a great amount of work, and the man whom nothing can make angry accomplishes so much. The man who gives way to anger, or hatred, or any other passion, cannot work; he only breaks himself to pieces, and does nothing practical. It is the calm, forgiving, equable, well-balanced mind that does the greatest amount of work.

Do not identify yourself with anything. Hold your mind free. All this that you see, the pains and the miseries, are but the necessary conditions of this world; poverty and wealth and happiness are but momentary; they do not belong to our real nature at all. Our nature is far beyond misery and happiness, beyond every object of the senses, beyond the imagination; and yet we must go on working all the time. "Misery comes through attachment, not through work." As soon as we identify ourselves with the work we do, we feel miserable; but if we do not identify ourselves with it, we do not feel that misery.

If a beautiful picture belonging to another is burnt, a man does not generally become miserable; but when his own picture is burnt, how miserable he feels! Why? Both were beautiful pictures, perhaps copies of the same original; but in one case very much more misery is felt than in the other. It is because in one case he identifies himself with the picture, and not in the other.

This "I and mine" causes the whole misery. With the sense of possession comes selfishness, and selfishness brings on misery. Every act of selfishness or thought of selfishness makes us attached to something, and immediately we are made slaves.

Therefore Karma-Yoga tells us to enjoy the beauty of all the pictures in the world, but not to identify ourselves with any of them. Never say "mine". Whenever we say a thing is "mine", misery will immediately come.

We all understand that desires are wrong, but what is meant by giving up desires? How could life go on? It would be the same suicidal advice, killing the desire and the man too. The solution is this. Not that you should not have property, not that you should not have things which are necessary and things which are even luxuries.

Have all that you want, and more, only know the truth and realise it. Wealth does not belong to anybody. Have no idea of proprietorship, possessorship. You are nobody, nor am I, nor anyone else.

All belongs to the Lord, because the opening verse told us to put the Lord in everything. God is in the wealth that you enjoy. He is in the desire that rises in your mind. He is in the things you buy to satisfy your desire; He is in your beautiful attire, in your beautiful ornaments. This is the line of thought.

All will be metamorphosed as soon as you begin to see things in that light. If you put God in your every movement, in your conversation, in your form, in everything, the whole scene changes, and the world, instead of appearing as one of woe and misery, will become a heaven.

"The kingdom of heaven is within you," says Jesus; so says the Vedanta, and every great teacher. "He that hath eyes to see, let him see, and he that hath ears to hear, let him hear." The Vedanta proves that the truth for which we have been searching all this time is present, and was all the time with us.

In our ignorance, we thought we had lost it, and went about the world crying and weeping, struggling to find the truth, while all along it was dwelling in our own hearts. There alone can we find it.

If we understand the giving up of the world in its old, crude sense, then it would come to this: that we must not work, that we must be idle, sitting like lumps of earth, neither thinking nor doing anything, but must become fatalists, driven about by every circumstance, ordered about by the laws of nature, drifting from place to place.

That would be the result. But that is not what is meant. We must work. Ordinary mankind, driven everywhere by false desire, what do they know of work? The man propelled by his own feelings and his own senses, what does he know about work? He works, who is not propelled by his own desires, by any selfishness whatsoever. He works, who has no ulterior motive in view. He works, who has nothing to gain from work.

Here are the two ways of giving up all attachment. The one is for those who do not believe in God, or in any outside help. They are left to their own devices; they have simply to work with their own will, with the powers of their mind and discrimination, saying, "I must be non-attached".

For those who believe in God there is another way, which is much less difficult. They give up the fruits of work unto the Lord; they work and are never attached to the results.

Whatever they see, feel, hear, or do, is for Him. For whatever good work we may do, let us not claim any praise or benefit. It is the Lord's; give up the fruits unto Him.

Let us stand aside and think that we are only servants obeying the Lord, our Master, and that every impulse for action comes from Him every moment. Whatever thou worshippest, whatever thou perceivest, whatever thou doest, give up all unto Him and be at rest.

Give up all desire and be at peace. Have neither friends nor foes, and live alone. Thus shall we travel having neither friends nor foes, neither pleasure nor pain, neither desire nor jealousy, injuring no creatures, being the cause of injury to no creatures — from mountain to mountain, from village to village, preaching the name of the Lord. Seek no help from high or low, from above or below. Desire nothing — and look upon this vanishing panorama as a witness and let it pass.

Give up all argumentation and other distractions. Is there anything in dry intellectual jargon? It only throws the mind off its balance and disturbs it.

Control the organs of the senses and control the mind. Bear every misery without even knowing that you are miserable. Think of nothing but liberation.

Combine seriousness with childlike naïveté . Live in harmony with all. Give up all idea of egoism, and entertain no sectarian views. Useless wrangling is a great sin.

Give up forever the desire for name and fame and power.

"Give up," says the Veda, "give up." That is the one way, "Give up".न प्रजया धनेन त्यागेनैकेऽमृतत्वमानशुः — "Neither through wealth, nor through progeny, but by giving up alone that immortality is to be reached."

Give up the burden of all deeds to the Lord; give all, both good and bad. Do not keep the good and give only the bad. God helps those who do not help themselves.

Weakness is the one cause of suffering. We become miserable because we are weak. We lie, steal, kill, and commit other crimes, because we are weak. We suffer because we are weak. We die because we are weak. Where there is nothing to weaken us, there is no death nor sorrow. We are miserable through delusion. Give up the delusion, and the whole thing vanishes. It is plain and simple indeed. Through all these philosophical discussions and tremendous mental gymnastics we come to this one religious idea, the simplest in the whole world.

You remember that passage in the sermon of Buddha, how he sent a thought of love towards the south, the north, the east, and the west, above and below, until the whole universe was filled with this lose, so grand, great, and infinite. When you have that feeling, you have true personality. The whole universe is one person; let go the little things. Give up the small for the Infinite, give up small enjoyments for infinite bliss.

Most of the religions understand the fact, but the error into which they all seem to fall is the same; they are carried away by the heart, the feelings. There is evil in the world, give up the world; that is the great teaching, and the only teaching, no doubt.

Give up the world. There cannot be two opinions that to understand the truth everyone of us has to give up error. There cannot be two opinions that everyone of us in order to have good must give up evil; there cannot be two opinions that everyone of us to have life must give up what is death.

And yet, what remains to us, if this theory involves giving up the life of the senses, the life as we know it? And what else do we mean by life? If we give this up, what remains?

In Vedanta alone we find a rational solution of the problem. Here I can only lay before you what the Vedanta seeks to teach, and that is the deification of the world. The Vedanta does not in reality denounce the world. The ideal of renunciation nowhere attains such a height as in the teachings of the Vedanta.

But, at the same time, dry suicidal advice is not intended; it really means deification of the world — giving up the world as we think of it, as we know it, as it appears to us — and to know what it really is. Deify it; it is God alone. We read at the commencement of one of the oldest of the Upanishads, "Whatever exists in this universe is to be covered with the Lord."

We have to cover everything with the Lord Himself, not by a false sort of optimism, not by blinding our eyes to the evil, but by really seeing God in everything. Thus we have to give up the world, and when the world is given up, what remains? God.

Renunciation of the senses and desires is the only way out of this misery. If you want to be spiritual, you must renounce. This is the real test. Give up the world — this nonsense of the senses. There is only one real desire: to know what is true, to be spiritual. No more materialism, no more this egoism, I must become spiritual.

Strong, intense must be the desire. If a man's hands and feet were so tied that he could not move and then if a burning piece of charcoal were placed on his body, he would struggle with all his power to throw it off. When I shall have that sort of extreme desire, that restless struggle, to throw off this burning world, then the time will have come for me to glimpse the Divine Truth.

Give up this little life of yours. What matters it if you die of starvation — you and I and thousands like us — so long as this nation lives? What matters it if this little life goes? Everyone has to die, the saint or the sinner, the rich or the poor. The body never remains for anyone. Arise and awake and be perfectly sincere. Give up your passive attitude, gird your loins and stand up.

The fact being that the Lord is in us, we are He, the eternal subject, the real ego, never to be objectified, and that all this objectifying process is mere waste of time and talent. When the soul becomes aware of this, it gives up objectifying and falls back more and more upon the subjective.

This is the evolution, less and less in the body and more and more in the mind — man the highest form, meaning in Sanskrit manas , thought — the animal that thinks and not the animal that "senses" only. This is what in theology is called "renunciation". The formation of society, the institution of marriage, the love for children, our good works, morality, and ethics are all different forms of renunciation.

All our lives in every society are the subjection of the will, the thirst, the desire. This surrender of the will or the fictitious self — or the desire to jump out of ourselves, as it were — the struggle still to objectify the subject — is the one phenomenon in this world of which all societies and social forms are various modes and stages. Love is the easiest and smoothest way towards the self-surrender or subjection of the will and hatred, the opposite.

Karma-Yoga is purifying the mind by means of work. Now if any work is done, good or bad, it must produce as a result a good or bad effect; no power can stay it, once the cause is present.

Therefore good action producing good Karma, and bad action, bad Karma, the soul will go on in eternal bondage without ever hoping for deliverance. Now Karma belongs only to the body or the mind, never to the Atman (Self); only it can cast a veil before the Atman.

The veil cast by bad Karma is ignorance. Good Karma has the power to strengthen the moral powers. And thus it creates non-attachment; it destroys the tendency towards bad Karma and thereby purifies the mind. But if the work is done with the intention of enjoyment, it then produces only that very enjoyment and does not purify the mind or Chitta.

Therefore all work should be done without any desire to enjoy the fruits thereof. All fear and all desire to enjoy here or hereafter must be banished for ever by the Karma-Yogi. Moreover, this Karma without desire of return will destroy the selfishness, which is the root of all bondage.

The watchword of the Karma-Yogi is "not I, but Thou", and no amount of self-sacrifice is too much for him. But he does this without any desire to go to heaven, or gain name or fame or any other benefit in this world.

Although the explanation and rationale of this unselfish work is only in Jnâna-Yoga, yet the natural divinity of man makes him love all sacrifice simply for the good of others, without any ulterior motive, whatever his creed or opinion. Again, with many the bondage of wealth is very great; and Karma-Yoga is absolutely necessary for them as breaking the crystallisation that has gathered round their love of money.

He is free, he is great, who turns his back upon the world, who has renounced everything, who has controlled his passion, and who thirsts for peace. One may gain political and social independence, but if one is a slave to his passions and desires, one cannot feel the pure joy of real freedom.

It is in the nature of work to be impelled ordinarily by motive and by attachment. In the presence of an ever active Providence who notes even the sparrow's fall, how can man attach any importance to his own work? Will it not be a blasphemy to do so when we know that He is taking care of the minutest things in the world?

We have only to stand in awe and reverence before Him saying, "Thy will be done". The highest men cannot work, for in them there is no attachment. Those whose whole soul is gone into the Self, those whose desires are confined in the Self, who have become ever associated with the Self, for them there is no work.

Such are indeed the highest of mankind; but apart from them every one else has to work. In so working we should never think that we can help on even the least thing in this universe. We cannot. We only help ourselves in this gymnasium of the world. This is the proper attitude of work. If we work in this way, if we always remember that our present opportunity to work thus is a privilege which has been given to us, we shall never be attached to anything.

Millions like you and me think that we are great people in the world; but we all die, and in five minutes the world forgets us. But the life of God is infinite. "Who can live a moment, breathe a moment, if this all-powerful One does not will it?"

He is the ever active Providence. All power is His and within His command. Through His command the winds blow, the sun shines, the earth lives, and death stalks upon the earth. He is the all in all; He is all and in all. We can only worship Him.

Give up all fruits of work; do good for its own sake; then alone will come perfect non-attachment. The bonds of the heart will thus break, and we shall reap perfect freedom. This freedom is indeed the goal of Karma-Yoga.

The Practice of Unattachment

Attachment is the source of all our pleasures now. We are attached to our friends, to our relatives; we are attached to our intellectual and spiritual works; we are attached to external objects, so that we get pleasure from them.

What, again, brings misery but this very attachment? We have to detach ourselves to earn joy. If only we had power to detach ourselves at will, there would not be any misery. That man alone will be able to get the best of nature, who, having the power of attaching himself to a thing with all his energy, has also the power to detach himself when he should do so.

The difficulty is that there must be as much power of attachment as that of detachment. There are men who are never attracted by anything. They can never love, they are hard-hearted and apathetic; they escape most of the miseries of life.

But the wall never feels misery, the wall never loves, is never hurt; but it is the wall, after all. Surely it is better to be attached and caught, than to be a wall. Therefore the man who never loves, who is hard and stony, escaping most of the miseries of life, escapes also its joys.

We do not want that. That is weakness, that is death. That soul has not been awakened that never feels weakness, never feels misery. That is a callous state. We do not want that.

At the same time, we not only want this mighty power of love, this mighty power of attachment, the power of throwing our whole soul upon a single object, losing ourselves and letting ourselves be annihilated, as it were, for other souls — which is the power of the gods — but we want to be higher even than the gods.

The perfect man can put his whole soul upon that one point of love, yet he is unattached. How comes this? There is another secret to learn.

The beggar is never happy. The beggar only gets a dole with pity and scorn behind it, at least with the thought behind that the beggar is a low object. He never really enjoys what he gets.

We are all beggars. Whatever we do, we want a return. We are all traders. We are traders in life, we are traders in virtue, we are traders in religion. And alas! we are also traders in love.

If you come to trade, if it is a question of give-and-take, if it is a question of buy-and-sell, abide by the laws of buying and selling. There is a bad time and there is a good time; there is a rise and a fall in prices: always you expect the blow to come. It is like looking at the mirrors Your face is reflected: you make a grimace — there is one in the mirror; if you laugh, the mirror laughs. This is buying and selling, giving and taking.

We get caught. How? Not by what we give, but by what we expect. We get misery in return for our love; not from the fact that we love, but from the fact that we want love in return.

There is no misery where there is no want. Desire, want, is the father of all misery. Desires are bound by the laws of success and failure.

Desires must bring misery.

The great secret of true success, of true happiness, then, is this: the man who asks for no return, the perfectly unselfish man, is the most successful. It seems to be a paradox. Do we not know that every man who is unselfish in life gets cheated, gets hurt? Apparently, yes. "Christ was unselfish, and yet he was crucified." True, but we know that his unselfishness is the reason, the cause of a great victory — the crowning of millions upon millions of lives with the blessings of true success.

Ask nothing; want nothing in return. Give what you have to give; it will come back to you — but do not think of that now, it will come back multiplied a thousandfold — but the attention must not be on that. Yet have the power to give: give, and there it ends. Learn that the whole of life is giving, that nature will force you to give.

So, give willingly. Sooner or later you will have to give up. You come into life to accumulate. With clenched hands, you want to take. But nature puts a hand on your throat and makes your hands open. Whether you will it or not, you have to give.

The moment you say, "I will not", the blow comes; you are hurt. None is there but will be compelled, in the long run, to give up everything.

And the more one struggles against this law, the more miserable one feels. It is because we dare not give, because we are not resigned enough to accede to this grand demand of nature, that we are miserable.

The forest is gone, but we get heat in return. The sun is taking up water from the ocean, to return it in showers. You are a machine for taking and giving: you take, in order to give.

Ask, therefore, nothing in return; but the more you give, the more will come to you. The quicker you can empty the air out of this room, the quicker it will be filled up by the external air; and if you close all the doors and every aperture, that which is within will remain, but that which is outside will never come in, and that which is within will stagnate, degenerate, and become poisoned.

A river is continually emptying itself into the ocean and is continually filling up again. Bar not the exit into the ocean. The moment you do that, death seizes you.

Be, therefore, not a beggar; be unattached. This is the most terrible task of life! You do not calculate the dangers on the path. Even by intellectually recognising the difficulties, we really do not know them until we feel them.

From a distance we may get a general view of a park: well, what of that? We feel and really know it when we are in it. Even if our every attempt is a failure, and we bleed and are torn asunder, yet, through all this, we have to preserve our heart — we must assert our Godhead in the midst of all these difficulties.

Nature wants us to react, to return blow for blow, cheating for cheating, lie for lie, to hit back with all our might. Then it requires a superdivine power not to hit back, to keep control, to be unattached.

Every day we renew our determination to be unattached. We cast our eyes back and look at the past objects of our love and attachment, and feel how every one of them made us miserable. We went down into the depths of despondency because of our "love"! We found ourselves mere slaves in the hands of others, we were dragged down and down!

And we make a fresh determination: "Henceforth, I will be master of myself; henceforth, I will have control over myself." But the time comes, and the same story once more! Again the soul is caught and cannot get out. The bird is in a net, struggling and fluttering. This is our life.

I know the difficulties. Tremendous they are, and ninety per cent of us become discouraged and lose heart, and in our turn, often become pessimists and cease to believe in sincerity, love, and all that is grand and noble.

So, we find men who in the freshness of their lives have been forgiving, kind, simple, and guileless, become in old age lying masks of men. Their minds are a mass of intricacy. There may be a good deal of external policy, possibly. They are not hot-headed, they do not speak, but it would be better for them to do so; their hearts are dead and, therefore, they do not speak.

They do not curse, not become angry; but it would be better for them to be able to be angry, a thousand times better, to be able to curse. They cannot. There is death in the heart, for cold hands have seized upon it, and it can no more act, even to utter a curse, even to use a harsh word.

All this we have to avoid: therefore I say, we require superdivine power. Superhuman power is not strong enough. Superdivine strength is the only way, the one way out. By it alone we can pass through all these intricacies, through these showers of miseries, unscathed. We may be cut to pieces, torn asunder, yet our hearts must grow nobler and nobler all the time.

It is very difficult, but we can overcome the difficulty by constant practice. We must learn that nothing can happen to us, unless we make ourselves susceptible to it. I have just said, no disease can come to me until the body is ready; it does not depend alone on the germs, but upon a certain predisposition which is already in the body. We get only that for which we are fitted.

Let us give up our pride and understand this, that never is misery undeserved. There never has been a blow undeserved: there never has been an evil for which I did not pave the way with my own hands. We ought to know that. Analyse yourselves and you will find that every blow you have received, came to you because you prepared yourselves for it. You did half, and the external world did the other half: that is how the blow came. That will sober us down.

At the same time, from this very analysis will come a note of hope, and the note of hope is: "I have no control of the external world, but that which is in me and nearer unto me, my own world, is in my control. If the two together are required to make a failure, if the two together are necessary to give me a blow, I will not contribute the one which is in my keeping; and how then can the blow come? If I get real control of myself, the blow will never come."

By non-attachment and practice, meditation is perfected.

"I cannot tell anything about Thee except that Thou art my love. Thou art beautiful, Oh, Thou art beautiful! Thou art beauty itself." What is after all really required of us in this Yoga is that our thirst after the beautiful should be directed to God. What is the beauty in the human face, in the sky, in the stars, and in the moon? It is only the partial apprehension of the real all-embracing Divine Beauty. "He shining, everything shines. It is through His light that all things shine."

Take this high position of Bhakti which makes you forget at once all your little personalities. Take yourself away from all the world's little selfish clingings. Do not look upon humanity as the centre of all your human and higher interests. Stand as a witness, as a student, and observe the phenomena of nature.

Have the feeling of personal non-attachment with regard to man, and see how this mighty feeling of love is working itself out in the world. Sometimes a little friction is produced, but that is only in the course of the struggle to attain the higher real love. Sometimes there is a little fight or a little fall; but it is all only by the way. Stand aside, and freely let these frictions come. You feel the frictions only when you are in the current of the world, but when you are outside of it simply as a witness and as a student, you will be able to see that there are millions and millions of channels in which God is manifesting Himself as Love.

The Bhakti-Yogi knows the meaning of life's struggles; he understands it. He has passed through a long series of these struggles and knows what they mean and earnestly desires to be free from the friction thereof; he wants to avoid the clash and go direct to the centre of all attraction, the great Hari.

This is the renunciation of the Bhakta. This mighty attraction in the direction of God makes all other attractions vanish for him. This mighty infinite love of God which enters his heart leaves no place for any other love to live there. How can it be otherwise? Bhakti fills his heart with the divine waters of the ocean of love, which is God Himself; there is no place there for little loves. That is to say, the Bhakta's renunciation is that Vairâgya or non-attachment for all things that are not God which results from Anurâga or great attachment to God.

Whenever we say a thing is "mine", misery will immediately come. Do not even say "my child" in your mind. Possess the child, but do not say "mine". If you do, then will come the misery.

Do not say "my house," do not say "my body". The whole difficulty is there. The body is neither yours, nor mine, nor anybody's. These bodies are coming and going by the laws of nature, but we are free, standing as witness.

This body is no more free than a picture or a wall. Why should we be attached so much to a body? If somebody paints a picture, he does it and passes on. Do not project that tentacle of selfishness, "I must possess it". As soon as that is projected, misery will begin.

So Karma-Yoga says, first destroy the tendency to project this tentacle of selfishness, and when you have the power of checking it, hold it in and do not allow the mind to get into the ways of selfishness. Then you may go out into the world and work as much as you can. Mix everywhere, go where you please; you will never be contaminated with evil. There is the lotus leaf in the water; the water cannot touch and adhere to it; so will you be in the world. This is called "Vairâgya", dispassion or non-attachment.

I believe I have told you that without non-attachment there cannot be any kind of Yoga. Non-attachment is the basis of all the Yogas. The man who gives up living in houses, wearing fine clothes, and eating good food, and goes into the desert, may be a most attached person. His only possession, his own body, may become everything to him; and as he lives he will be simply struggling for the sake of his body.

Non-attachment does not mean anything that we may do in relation to our external body, it is all in the mind. The binding link of "I and mine" is in the mind. If we have not this link with the body and with the things of the senses, we are non-attached, wherever and whatever we may be. A man may be on a throne and perfectly non-attached; another man may be in rags and still very much attached.

First, we have to attain this state of non-attachment and then to work incessantly. Karma-Yoga gives us the method that will help us in giving up all attachment, though it is indeed very hard.

The body is our enemy, and yet is our friend. Which of you can bear the sight of misery? And which of you cannot do so when you see it only as a painting? Because it is unreal, we do not identify ourselves with it, eve know it is only a painting; it cannot bless us, it cannot hurt us.

The most terrible misery painted upon a price of canvas, we may even enjoy; we praise the technique of the artist, we wonder at his marvellous genius, even though the scene he paints is most horrible. That is the secret; that non-attachment. Be the Witness.

Since I was a child I have heard about Krishna's life. I take it for granted there must have been a man called Krishna, and his Gita shows he has left a wonderful book.

I told you, you can understand the character of a man by analysing the fables about him. The fables have the nature [of decorations]. You must find they are all polished and manipulated to fit into the character.

For instance, take Buddha. The central idea [is] sacrifice. There are thousands of folklore, but in every case the sacrifice must have been kept up.

There are thousands of stories about Lincoln, about some characteristic of that great man. You take all the fables and find the general idea and [know] that that was the central character of the man.

You find in Krishna that non-attachment is the central idea. He does not need anything. He does not want anything. He works for work's sake. "Work for work's sake. Worship for worship's sake. Do good because it is good to do good. Ask no more."

That must have been the character of the man. Otherwise these fables could not be brought down to the one idea of non-attachment.

The purer the body and mind, the quicker the desired result will be obtained. You must be perfectly pure. Do not think of evil things, such thoughts will surely drag you down.

If you are perfectly pure and practice faithfully, your mind can finally be made a searchlight of infinite power. There is no limit to its scope.

But there must be constant practice and non-attachment to the world. When a man reaches the superconscious state, all feeling of body melts away. Then alone does he become free and immortal.

Temporal Enjoyments

Whatever work we do, the mind is thrown into a wave, and after the work is finished, we think the wave is gone. No. It has only become fine, but it is still there. When we try to remember the work, it comes up again and becomes a wave. So it was there; if not, there would not have been memory.

Thus every action, every thought, good or bad, just goes down and becomes fine, and is there stored up. Both happy and unhappy thoughts are called pain-bearing obstructions, because according to the Yogis, they, in the long run, bring pain.

All happiness which comes from the senses will, eventually, bring pain. All enjoyment will make us thirst for more, and that brings pain as its result. There is no limit to man's desires; he goes on desiring, and when he comes to a point where desire cannot be fulfilled, the result is pain.

Therefore the Yogis regard the sum-total of the impressions, good or evil, as pain-bearing obstructions; they obstruct the way to freedom of the Soul.

The first ideal of the attempt to realise religion is that of renunciation. As far as we can, we must give up. Darkness and light, enjoyment of the world and enjoyment of God will never go together. "Ye cannot serve God and Mammon." Let people try it if they will, and I have seen millions in every country who have tried; but after all, it comes to nothing.

If one word remains true in the saying, it is, give up everything for the sake of the Lord. This is a hard and long task, but you can begin it here and now. Bit by bit we must go towards it.

The goal of man is to go beyond law. And enjoyment can never be the goal, because enjoyment can only be in nature. Alas, alas, the desire for enjoyment does not leave a man.

Enjoyment, misery, luxury, wealth, power, and poverty, even life itself, are all evanescent.

Everything that has selfishness for its basis, competition as its right hand, and enjoyment as its goal, must die sooner or later. Such things must die.

Enjoyment is the million-headed serpent that we must tread under foot. We renounce and go on, then find nothing and despair; but hold on, hold on . The world is a demon. It is a kingdom of which the puny ego is king.

Put it away and stand firm. Give up lust and gold and fame and hold fast to the Lord, and at last we shall reach a state of perfect indifference. The idea that the gratification of the senses constitutes enjoyment is purely materialistic. There is not one spark of real enjoyment there; all the joy there is, is a mere reflection of the true bliss.

Plunder and fight as you may, the enjoyment that you are seeking is only in peace; and peace, in the renunciation of physical pleasures. Enjoyment lies not in physical development, but in the culture of the mind and the intellect.

Is enjoyment the goal of life? Were it so, it would be a tremendous mistake to become a man at all. What man can enjoy a meal with more gusto than the dog or the cat ? Go to a menagerie and see the wild animals tearing the flesh from the bone. Go back and become a bird! What a mistake then to become a man! Vain have been my years — hundreds of years — of struggle only to become the man of sense-enjoyments.

What is the goal of it all? Can senses ever be the goal? Can enjoyment of pleasure ever be the goal? Can this life ever be the goal of the soul? If it is, better die this moment; do not want this life! If that is the fate of man, that he is going to be only the perfected machine, it would just mean that we go back to being trees and stones and things like that.

Did you ever hear a cow tell a lie or see a tree steal? They are perfect machines. They do not make mistakes. They live in a world where everything is finished.

So long as enjoyment is sought, bondage remains. Only imperfection can enjoy, because enjoyment is the fulfilling of desire. The human soul enjoys nature. The underlying reality of nature, soul, and God is Brahman; but It (Brahman) is unseen, until we bring It out.

It may be brought out by Pramantha or friction, just as we can produce fire by friction. The body is the lower piece of wood, Om is the pointed piece and Dhyâna (meditation) is the friction. When this is used, that light which is the knowledge of Brahman will burst forth in the soul.

The lower the animal, the more is its enjoyment in the senses, the more it lives in the senses. Civilisation, true civilization, should mean the power of taking the animal-man out of his sense-life — by giving him visions and tastes of planes much higher — and not external comforts.

Man knows this instinctively. He may not formulate it to himself under all circumstances. He may form very divergent opinions about the life of thought. But it is there, pressing itself to the front in spite of everything, making him pay reverence to the hoodoo-worker, the medicine-man, the magician, the priest, or the professor of science.

The growth of man can only be gauged by his power of living in the higher atmosphere where the senses are left behind, the amount of the pure thought-oxygen his lungs can breathe in, and the amount of time he can spend on that height.

As it is, it is an obvious fact that, with the exception of what is taken up by the necessities of life, the man of culture is loth to spend his time on so-called comforts, and even necessary actions are performed with lessened zeal, as the process moves forward.

The other great mistake we often make is that good is taken as an ever-increasing item, whilst evil is a fixed quantity. From this it is argued that evil being diminished every day, there will come a time when good alone will remain.

The fallacy lies in the assumption of a false premise. If good is increasing, so is evil. My desires have been much more than the desires of the masses among my race. My joys have been much greater than theirs — but my miseries a million times more intense. The same constitution that makes you feel the least touch of good makes you feel the least of evil too. The same nerves that carry sensations of pleasure carry the sensations of pain too — and the same mind feels both.

The progress of the world means more enjoyment and more misery too. This mixture of life and death, good and evil, knowledge and ignorance is what is called Maya — or the universal phenomenon.

You may go on for eternity inside this net, seeking for happiness — you find much, and much evil too. To have good and no evil is childish nonsense.

Two ways are left open — one by giving up all hope to take up the world as it is and bear the pangs and pains in the hope of a crumb of happiness now and then. The other, to give up the search for pleasure, knowing it to be pain in another form, and seek for truth — and those that dare try for truth succeed in finding that truth as ever present — present in themselves.

Then we also discover how the same truth is manifesting itself both in our relative error and knowledge — we find also that the same truth is bliss which again is manifesting itself as good and evil, and with it also we find real existence which is manifesting itself as both death and life.

Nowadays people among the backward nations, and among the less cultured portion of the civilised people of the West are laying much stress on the non-essential. Among the cultured and the wealthy, matters are on a different footing. The wealthy are either immersed in the enjoyment of health or grubbing for more. They, and a large section of the busy people, say of religion that it is rot, stuff, nonsense, and they honestly think so.

There never was a person who found happiness in the senses or in enjoyment of the senses. The world is our fish basket, we must not depend upon it for enjoyment. This is a place for action, not enjoyment.

Through enjoyment Yoga will come in time. But alas, such is the lot of my countrymen that, not to speak of possessing yoga, they cannot even have a little Bhoga! Suffering all sorts of indignities they can with the utmost difficulty only meet the barest needs of the body—and even that everyone cannot do! It is strange that such a state of affairs does not disturb our sleep and rouse us to our immediate duties.

To the vast majority of mankind, the body is everything; the body is all the universe to them; bodily enjoyment is their all in all. This demon of the worship of the body and of the things of the body has entered into us all. We may indulge in tall talk and take very high flights, but we are like vultures all the same; our mind is directed to the piece of carrion down below.

Why should our body be saved, say, from the tiger? Why may we not give it over to the tiger? The tiger will thereby be pleased, and that is not altogether so very far from self-sacrifice and worship.

Can you reach the realization of such an idea in which all sense of self is completely lost? It is a very dizzy height on the pinnacle of the religion of love, and few in this world have ever climbed up to it; but until a man reaches that highest point of ever-ready and ever-willing self-sacrifice, he cannot become a perfect Bhakta.

We may all manage to maintain our bodies more or less satisfactorily and for longer or shorter intervals of time. Nevertheless, our bodies have to go; there is no permanence about them. Blessed are they whose bodies get destroyed in the service of others.

"Wealth, and even life itself, the sage always holds ready for the service of others. In this world, there being one thing certain, viz death, it is far better that this body dies in a good cause than in a bad one."

We may drag our life on for fifty years or a hundred years; but after that, what is it that happens? Everything that is the result of combination must get dissolved and die. There must and will come a time for it to be decomposed. Jesus and Buddha and Mohammed are all dead; all the great Prophets and Teachers of the world are dead.

The history of the world shows that evil is a continuously increasing quantity, as well as good. Take the lowest man; he lives in the forest. His sense of enjoyment is very small, and so also is his power to suffer.

His misery is entirely on the sense-plane. If he does not get plenty of food, he is miserable; but give him plenty of food and freedom to rove and to hunt, and he is perfectly happy. His happiness consists only in the senses, and so does his misery also.

But if that man increases in knowledge, his happiness will increase, the intellect will open to him, and his sense-enjoyment will evolve into intellectual enjoyment. He will feel pleasure in reading a beautiful poem, and a mathematical problem will be of absorbing interest to him. But, with these, the inner nerves will become more and more susceptible to miseries of mental pain, of which the savage does not think.

Take a very simple illustration. In Tibet there is no marriage, and there is no jealousy, yet we know that marriage is a much higher state. The Tibetans have not known the wonderful enjoyment, the blessing of chastity, the happiness of having a chaste, virtuous wife, or a chaste, virtuous husband. These people cannot feel that.

And similarly they do not feel the intense jealousy of the chaste wife or husband, or the misery caused by unfaithfulness on either side, with all the heart-burnings and sorrows which believers in chastity experience. On one side, the latter gain happiness, but on the other, they suffer misery too.

Desire Will Bring Misery

Desire is infinite. Its fulfilment is very limited. There is no end to our desires; but when we go to fulfil them, the difficulty comes. It has been so with the most primitive minds, when their desires were few. Even these could not be accomplished.

Now, with our arts and sciences improved and multiplied, our desires cannot be fulfilled [either]. On the other hand, we are struggling to perfect means for the fulfilment of desires, and the desires are increasing.

Thirst for happiness being eternal, desires are without beginning.

All experience is preceded by desire for happiness. There was no beginning of experience, as each fresh experience is built upon the tendency generated by past experience; therefore desire is without beginning.

Desires are held together by cause and effect; if a desire has been raised, it does not die without producing its effect. Then, again, the mind-stuff is the great storehouse, the support of all past desires reduced to Samskāra form; until they have worked themselves out, they will not die.

Moreover, so long as the senses receive the external objects, fresh desires will arise. If it be possible to get rid of the cause, effect, support, and objects of desire, then alone it will vanish.

We get misery in return for our love; not from the fact that we love, but from the fact that we want love in return. There is no misery where there is no want. Desire, want, is the father of all misery. Desires are bound by the laws of success and failure. Desires must bring misery.

What makes us all struggle for something beyond what we see — whether it be a beautiful morning or a fear of dead spirits? We need not go back into prehistoric times, for it is a fact present today as it was two thousand years ago. We do not find satisfaction here. Whatever our station in life — even if we are powerful and wealthy — we cannot find satisfaction.

Desire is infinite. Its fulfilment is very limited. There is no end to our desires; but when we go to fulfil them, the difficulty comes. It has been so with the most primitive minds, when their desires were few. Even these could not be accomplished. Now, with our arts and sciences improved and multiplied, our desires cannot be fulfilled either. On the other hand, we are struggling to perfect means for the fulfilment of desires, and the desires are increasing.

Many want pleasure as the goal. For that pleasure they seek only the senses. On the higher planes much pleasure is to be sought. Then on spiritual planes. Then in himself — God within him. The man whose pleasure is outside of himself becomes unhappy when that outside thing goes.

You cannot depend for this pleasure upon anything in this universe. If all my pleasures are in myself, I must have pleasure all the time because I can never lose my Self. Mother, father, child, wife, body, wealth — everything I can lose except my self. All desire is contained in the Self. This is individuality which never changes, and this is perfect.

And how to get it? They find what the great souls of this world — all great men and women — found. They all had the one truth, that this false individuality must go.

So this ego — the less there is of it, the nearer I am to that which I really am: the universal body. The less I think of my own individual mind, the nearer I am to that universal mind. The less I think of my own soul, the nearer I am to the universal soul.

We live in one body. We have some pain, some pleasure. Just for this little pleasure we have by living in this body, we are ready to kill everything in the universe to preserve ourselves.

If we had two bodies, would not that be much better? So on and on to bliss. I am in everybody. Through all hands I work; through all feet I walk. I speak through every mouth; I live in every body. Infinite my bodies, infinite my minds. I lived in Jesus of Nazareth, in Buddha, in Mohammed — in all the great and good of the past, of the present. I am going to live in all that may come afterwards. Is that theory No, it is the truth.

If you can realise this, how infinitely more pleasurable that will be. What an ecstasy of joy! Which one body is so great that we need here anything [of] the bodyAfter living in all the bodies of others, all the bodies there are in this world, what becomes of us? [We become one with the Infinite. And] that is the goal. That is the only way. One [man] says, "If I know the truth, I shall be melted away like butter." I wish people would be, but they are too tough to be melted so quickly!

The Jivanmukta ('the living free' or one who knows) alone is able to give real love, real charity, real truth, and it is truth alone that makes us free. Desire makes slaves of us, it is an insatiable tyrant and gives its victims no rest; but the Jivanmukta has conquered all desire by rising to the knowledge that he is the One and there is nothing left to wish for.

The mind brings before us all our delusions — body, sex, creed, caste, bondage; so we have to tell the truth to the mind incessantly, until it is made to realise it. Our real nature is all bliss, and all the pleasure we know is but a reflection, an atom, of that bliss we get from touching our real nature.

That is beyond both pleasure and pain. It is the "witness" of the universe, the unchanging reader before whom turn the leaves of the book of life.

Through practice comes Yoga, through Yoga comes knowledge, through knowledge love, and through love bliss.

There is a limit to the working power of human beings, but no limit to desire; so we strive to get hold of the working powers of others and enjoy the fruits of their labours, escaping work ourselves. Inventing machinery to work for us can never increase well-being, for in gratifying desire, we only find it, and then we want more and more without end.

Dying, still filled with ungratified desires, we have to be born again and again in the vain search for satisfaction. "Eight Millions of bodies have we had, before we reached the human", say the Hindus. Jnana says, "Kill desire and so get rid of it". That is the only way.

This world is not for cowards. Do not try to fly. Look not for success or failure. Join yourself to the perfectly unselfish will and work on. Know that the mind which is born to succeed joins itself to a determined will and perseveres. You have the right to work, but do not become so degenerate as to look for results.

Work incessantly, but see something behind the work. Even good deeds can find a man in great bondage. Therefore be not bound by good deeds or by desire for name and fame. Those who know this secret pass beyond this round of birth and death and become immortal.

The ordinary Sannyâsin gives up the world, goes out, and thinks of God. The real Sannyâsin lives in the world, but is not of it. Those who deny themselves, live in the forest, and chew the cud of unsatisfied desires are not true renouncers. Live in the midst of the battle of life. Anyone can keep calm in a cave or when asleep. Stand in the whirl and madness of action and reach the Centre. If you have found the Centre, you cannot be moved.

Our best work is done, our greatest influence is exerted, when we are without thought of self. All great geniuses know this. Let us open ourselves to the one Divine Actor, and let Him act, and do nothing ourselves.

"O Arjuna! I have no duty in the whole world ", says Krishna. Be perfectly resigned, perfectly unconcerned; then alone can you do any true work. No eyes can see the real forces, we can only see the results.

Put out self, lose it, forget it; just let God work, it is His business. We have nothing to do but stand aside and let God work. The more we go away, the more God comes in. Get rid of the little "I", and let only the great "I" live.

Desire nothing; think of God and look for no return. It is the desireless who bring results. The begging monks carry religion to every man's door; but they think that they do nothing, they claim nothing, their work is unconsciously done. If they should eat of the tree of knowledge, they would become egoists, and all the good they do would fly away.

As soon as we say "I", we are humbugged all the time; and we call it "knowable", but it is only going round and round like a bullock tied to a tree. The Lord has hidden Himself best, and His work is best; so he who hides himself best, accomplishes most. Conquer yourself , and the whole universe is yours.

Disciplineline as an Ideal

The Hindu Ideal of life is Nivarti; it means subjugation and conquest of evil passions, of nature of lust, revenge and avarice.

It does not mean conquest of all desire. It means only the annihilation of gross desires.

Every man is bound to love and sympathize with his fellow-creatures. A Sanyasi is one who has vanquished all his selfish passions and vowed to devote his life for the good of others. He loves all.

Sanyasis ought to be fed. They are not like the Christian bishops and Archbishops who must be paid to do their work with thousands of pounds per annum; all whose earnings are spent upon their own luxury — their wife and children.

The Sanyasi wants only a morsel of food, and then he places all his knowledge and services at the disposal of the public. He is a wandering missionary. Individuals and society have to work themselves up from "brute through man, into divine".

Even the lowest of the Hindus, the Pariah, has less of the brute in him than a Briton in a similar social status. This is the result of an old and excellent religious civilization. This evolution to a higher spiritual state is possible only through discipline and education.

Sometimes it is a good discipline to be forced to work for work's sake, even to the length of not being allowed to enjoy the fruits of one's labour.

Our motherland is a glowing example of the results and consequence of the eternal subjection of the individual to society and forced self-sacrifice by dint of institution and discipline.

In this country men are born according to Shâstric injunctions, they eat and drink by prescribed rules throughout life, they go through marriage and kindred functions in the same way; in short, they even die according to Shastric injunctions. The hard discipline, with the exception of one great good point, is fraught with evil.

The good point is that men can do one or two things well with very little effort, having practiced them every day through generations. The delicious rice and curry which a cook of this country prepares with the aid of three lumps of earth and a few sticks can be had nowhere else. With the simple mechanism of an antediluvian loom, worth one rupee, and the feet put in a pit, it is possible to make kincobs worth twenty rupees a yard, in this country alone.

A torn mat, an earthen lamp, and that fed by castor oil — with the aid of materials such as these, wonderful savants are produced in this country alone. An all-forbearing attachment to an ugly and deformed wife, and a lifelong devotion to a worthless and villainous husband are possible in this country alone. Thus far the bright side.

But all these things are done by people guided like lifeless machines. There is no mental activity, no unfoldment of the heart, no vibration of life, no flux of hope; there is no strong stimulation of the will, no experience of keen pleasure, nor the contact of intense sorrow; there is no stir of inventive genius, no desire for novelty, no appreciation of new things.

Clouds never pass away from this mind; the radiant picture of the morning sun never charms this heart. It never even occurs to this mind if there is any better state than this; where it does, it cannot convince; in the event of conviction, effort is lacking; and even where there is effort, lack of enthusiasm kills it out.

If living by rule alone ensures excellence, if it be virtue to follow strictly the rules and customs handed down through generations, say then, who is more virtuous than a tree, who is a greater devotee, a holier saint, than a railway train? Who has ever seen a piece of stone transgress a natural law? Who has ever known cattle to commit sin?

Again, can that be called society which is formed by an aggregate of men who are like lumps of clay, like lifeless machines, like heaped up pebbles? How can such society fare well? Were good possible, then instead of being slaves for hundreds of years, we would have been the greatest nation on earth, and this soil of India, instead of being a mine of stupidity, would have been the eternal fountain-head of learning.

The Idea of Maya

The theory of Maya forms one of the pillars upon which the Vedanta rests; it is, therefore, necessary that it should be properly understood. I ask a little patience of you, for there is a great danger of its being misunderstood.

The oldest idea of Maya that we find in Vedic literature is the sense of delusion; but then the real theory had not been reached. We find such passages as, "Indra through his Maya assumed various forms." Here it is true the word Maya means something like magic, and we find various other passages, always taking the same meaning. The word Maya then dropped out of sight altogether.

But in the meantime the idea was developing. Later, the question was raised: "Why can't we know this secret of the universe?" And the answer given was very significant: "Because we talk in vain, and because we are satisfied with the things of the senses, and because we are running after desires; therefore, we, as it were, cover the Reality with a mist."

Here the word Maya is not used at all, but we get the idea that the cause of our ignorance is a kind of mist that has come between us and the Truth. Much later on, in one of the latest Upanishads, we find the word Maya reappearing, but this time, a transformation has taken place in it, and a mass of new meaning has attached itself to the word.

Theories had been propounded and repeated, others had been taken up, until at last the idea of Maya became fixed. We read in the Shvetâshvatara Upanishad, "Know nature to be Maya and the Ruler of this Maya is the Lord Himself."

Coming to our philosophers, we find that this word Maya has been manipulated in various fashions, until we come to the great Shankarâchârya. The theory of Maya was manipulated a little by the Buddhists too, but in the hands of the Buddhists it became very much like what is called Idealism, and that is the meaning that is now generally given to the word Maya.

When the Hindu says the world is Maya, at once people get the idea that the world is an illusion. This interpretation has some basis, as coming through the Buddhistic philosophers, because there was one section of philosophers who did not believe in the external world at all. But the Maya of the Vedanta, in its last developed form, is neither Idealism nor Realism, nor is it a theory. It is a simple statement of facts — what we are and what we see around us.

The theory of Mâyâ is as old as the Rik-Samhitâ. The Shvetâshvatara Upanishad contains the word "Maya" which is developed out of Prakriti.

A legend tells how once Nârada said to Krishna, "Lord, show me Maya." A few days passed away, and Krishna asked Narada to make a trip with him towards a desert, and after walking for several miles, Krishna said, "Narada, I am thirsty; can you fetch some water for me?" "I will go at once, sir, and get you water."

So Narada went. At a little distance there was a village; he entered the village in search of water and knocked at a door, which was opened by a most beautiful young girl. At the sight of her he immediately forgot that his Master was waiting for water, perhaps dying for the want of it. He forgot everything and began to talk with the girl. All that day he did not return to his Master.

The next day, he was again at the house, talking to the girl. That talk ripened into love; he asked the father for the daughter, and they were married and lived there and had children.

Thus twelve years passed. His father-in-law died, he inherited his property. He lived, as he seemed to think, a very happy life with his wife and children, his fields and his cattle and so forth.

Then came a flood. One night the river rose until it overflowed its banks and flooded the whole village. Houses fell, men and animals were swept away and drowned, and everything was floating in the rush of the stream. Narada had to escape. With one hand be held his wife, and with the other two of his children; another child was on his shoulders, and he was trying to ford this tremendous flood.

After a few steps he found the current was too strong, and the child on his shoulders fell and was borne away. A cry of despair came from Narada. In trying to save that child, he lost his grasp upon one of the others, and it also was lost. At last his wife, whom he clasped with all his might, was torn away by the current, and he was thrown on the bank, weeping and wailing in bitter lamentation.

Behind him there came a gentle voice, "My child, where is the water? You went to fetch a pitcher of water, and I am waiting for you; you have been gone for quite half an hour." "Half an hour! " Narada exclaimed. Twelve whole years had passed through his mind, and all these scenes had happened in half an hour! And this is Maya.

Reformers arise and preach that learning, wealth, and culture should not be in the hands of a select few; and they do their best to make them accessible to all. These may bring more happiness to some, but, perhaps, as culture comes, physical happiness lessens. The knowledge of happiness brings the knowledge of unhappiness.

Which way then shall we go? The least amount of material prosperity that we enjoy is causing the same amount of misery elsewhere. This is the law. The young, perhaps, do not see it clearly, but those who have lived long enough and those who have struggled enough will understand it. And this is Maya.

These things are going on, day and night, and to find a solution of this problem is impossible. Why should it be so? It is impossible to answer this, because the question cannot be logically formulated. There is neither how nor why in fact; we only know that it is and that we cannot help it. Even to grasp it, to draw an exact image of it in our own mind, is beyond our power. How can we solve it then?

Maya is a statement of the fact of this universe, of how it is going on. People generally get frightened when these things are told to them. But bold we must be. Hiding facts is not the way to find a remedy.

As you all know, a hare hunted by dogs puts its head down and thinks itself safe; so, when we run into optimism; we do just like the hare, but that is no remedy. There are objections against this, but you may remark that they are generally from people who possess many of the good things of life. In this country (England) it is very difficult to become a pessimist.

Everyone tells me how wonderfully the world is going on, how progressive; but what he himself is, is his own world. Old questions arise: Christianity must be the only true religion of the world because Christian nations are prosperous! But that assertion contradicts itself, because the prosperity of the Christian nation depends on the misfortune of non-Christian nations. There must be some to prey on.

Suppose the whole world were to become Christian, then the Christian nations would become poor, because there would be no non-Christian nations for them to prey upon. Thus the argument kills itself. Animals are living upon plants, men upon animals and, worst of all, upon one another, the strong upon the weak. This is going on everywhere. And this is Maya.

What solution do you find for this? We hear every day many explanations, and are told that in the long run all will be good. Taking it for granted that this is possible, why should there be this diabolical way of doing good?

Why cannot good be done through good, instead of through these diabolical methods? The descendants of the human beings of today will be happy; but why must there be all this suffering now? There is no solution. This is Maya.

Again, we often hear that it is one of the features of evolution that it eliminates evil, and this evil being continually eliminated from the world, at last only good will remain. That is very nice to hear, and it panders to the vanity of those who have enough of this world's goods, who have not a hard struggle to face every day and are not being crushed under the wheel of this so-called evolution. It is very good and comforting indeed to such fortunate ones. The common herd may surfer, but they do not care; let them die, they are of no consequence.

Very good, yet this argument is fallacious from beginning to end. It takes for granted, in the first place, that manifested good and evil in this world are two absolute realities. In the second place, it make, at still worse assumption that the amount of good is an increasing quantity and the amount of evil is a decreasing quantity.

So, if evil is being eliminated in this way by what they call evolution, there will come a time when all this evil will be eliminated and what remains will be all good. Very easy to say, but can it be proved that evil is a lessening quantity?

Take, for instance, the man who lives in a forest, who does not know how to cultivate the mind, cannot read a book, has not heard of such a thing as writing. If he is severely wounded, he is soon all right again; while we die if we get a scratch. Machines are making things cheap, making for progress and evolution, but millions are crushed, that one may become rich; while one becomes rich, thousands at the same time become poorer and poorer, and whole masses of human beings are made slaves.

That way it is going on. The animal man lives in the senses. If he does not get enough to eat, he is miserable; or if something happens to his body, he is miserable. In the senses both his misery and his happiness begin and end. As soon as this man progresses, as soon as his horizon of happiness increases, his horizon of unhappiness increases proportionately.

The man in the forest does not know what it is to be jealous, to be in the law courts, to pay taxes, to be blamed by society, to be ruled over day and night by the most tremendous tyranny that human diabolism ever invented, which pries into the secrets of every human heart. He does not know how man becomes a thousand times more diabolical than any other animal, with all his vain knowledge and with all his pride.

Thus it is that, as we emerge out of the senses, we develop higher powers of enjoyment, and at the same time we have to develop higher powers of suffering too. The nerves become finer and capable off more suffering. In every society, we often find that the ignorant, common man, when abused, does not feel much, but he feels a good thrashing.

But the gentleman cannot bear a single word of abuse; he has become so finely nerved. Misery has increased with his susceptibility to happiness. This does not go much to prove the evolutionist's case.

As we increase our power to be happy, we also increase our power to suffer, and sometimes I am inclined to think that if we increase our power to become happy in arithmetical progression, we shall increase, on the other hand, our power to become miserable in geometrical progression. We who are progressing know that the more we progress, the more avenues are opened to pain as well as to pleasure. And this is Maya.

Thus we find that Maya is not a theory for the explanation of the world; it is simply a statement of facts as they exist, that the very basis of our being is contradiction, that everywhere we have to move through this tremendous contradiction, that wherever there is good, there must also be evil, and wherever there is evil, there must be some good, wherever there is life, death must follow as its shadow, and everyone who smiles will have to weep, and vice versa.

Nor can this state of things be remedied. We may verily imagine that there will be a place where there will be only good and no evil, where we shall only smile and never weep. This is impossible in the very nature of things; for the conditions will remain the same. Wherever there is the power of producing a smile in us, there lurks the power of producing tears. Wherever there is the power of producing happiness, there lurks somewhere the power of making us miserable.

As long as we recognise duality, or separate God and man, so long we must see good and evil. Only by going to the centre, by unifying ourselves with God can we escape the delusions of the senses.

When we let go the eternal fever of desire, the endless thirst that gives us no rest, when we have for ever quenched desire, we shall escape both good and evil, because we shall have transcended both. The satisfaction of desire only increases it, as oil poured on fire but makes it burn more fiercely.

The further from the centre, the faster goes the wheel, the less the rest. Draw near the centre, check desire, stamp it out, let the false self go, then our vision will clear and we shall see God.

Only through renunciation of this life and of all life to come (heaven etc.), can we reach the point where we stand firmly on the true Self. While we hope for anything, desire still rules us. Be for one moment really "hopeless", and the mist will clear.

For what to hope when one is the all of existence? The secret of Jnana is to give up all and be sufficient unto ourselves. Say "not", and you become "not"; say "is", and you become "is". Worship the Self within, naught else exists. All that binds us is Mâyâ-delusion.

When one is in ignorance, he sees the phenomenon and does not see God. When he sees God, this universe vanishes entirely for him. Ignorance or Mâyâ, as it is called, is the cause of all this phenomenon — the Absolute, the Unchangeable, being taken as this manifested universe.

This Maya is not absolute zero, nor non-existence. It is defined as neither existence nor non-existence. It is not existence, because that can be said only of the Absolute, the Unchangeable, and in this sense, Maya is non-existence.

Again, it cannot be said it is non-existence; for if it were, it could never produce phenomenon. So it is something which is neither; and in the Vedanta philosophy it is called Anirvachaniya or inexpressible.

Maya, then, is the real cause of this universe. Maya gives the name and form to what Brahman or God gives the material; and the latter seems to have been transformed into all this.

The Advaitists, then, have no place for the individual soul. They say individual souls are created by Maya. In reality they cannot exist. If there were only one existence throughout, how could it be that I am one, and you are one, and so forth?

We are all one, and the cause of evil is the perception of duality. As soon as I begin to feel that I am separate from this universe, then first comes fear, and then comes misery. "Where one hears another, one sees another, that is small. Where one does not see another, where one does not hear another, that is the greatest, that is God. In that greatest is perfect happiness. In small things there is no happiness."

Everyone is as much bound in thought, word, deed, and mind, as a piece of stone or this table. That I talk to you now is as rigorous in causation as that you listen to me. There is no freedom until you go beyond Maya. That is the real freedom of the soul. Men, however sharp and intellectual, however clearly they see the force of the logic that nothing here can be free, are all compelled to think they are free; they cannot help it.

No work can go on until we begin to say we are free. It means that the freedom we talk about is the glimpse of the blue sky through the clouds and that the real freedom — the blue sky itself — is behind.

True freedom cannot exist in the midst of this delusion, this hallucination, this nonsense of the world, this universe of the senses, body, and mind. All these dreams, without beginning or end, uncontrolled and uncontrollable, ill-adjusted, broken, inharmonious, form our idea of this universe.

In a dream, when you see a giant with twenty heads chasing you, and you are flying from him, you do not think it is inharmonious; you think it is proper and right. So is this law. All that you call law is simply chance without meaning. In this dream state you call it law.

Within Maya, so far as this law of time, space and causation exists, there is no freedom; and all these various forms of worship are within this Maya. The idea of God and the ideas of brute and of man are within this Maya, and as such are equally hallucinations; all of them are dreams.

But you must take care not to argue like some extraordinary men of whom we hear at the present time. They say the idea of God is a delusion, but the idea of this world is true. Both ideas stand or fall by the same logic. He alone has the right to be an atheist who denies this world, as well as the other.

The same argument is for both. The same mass of delusion extends from God to the lowest animal, from a blade of grass to the Creator. They stand or fall by the same logic. The same person who sees falsity in the idea of God ought also to see it in the idea of his own body or his own mind.

When God vanishes, then also vanish the body and mind; and when both vanish, that which is the Real Existence remains for ever. "There the eyes cannot go, nor the speech, nor the mind. We cannot see it, neither know it."

And we now understand that so far as speech and thought and knowledge and intellect go, it is all within this Maya within bondage. Beyond that is Reality. There neither thought, nor mind, nor speech, can reach.

So far it is intellectually all right, but then comes the practice. The real work is in the practice.

Are any practices necessary to realise this Oneness? Most decidedly. It is not that you become this Brahman. You are already that. It is not that you are going to become God or perfect; you are already perfect; and whenever you think you are not, it is a delusion. This delusion which says that you are Mr. So-and-so or Mrs. So-and-so can be got rid of by another delusion, and that is practice.

Fire will eat fire, and you can use one delusion to conquer another delusion. One cloud will come and brush away another cloud, and then both will go away.

What are these practices then? We must always bear in mind that we are not going to be free, but are free already. Every idea that we are bound is a delusion. Every idea that we are happy or unhappy is a tremendous delusion; and another delusion will come — that we have got to work and worship and struggle to be free — and this will chase out the first delusion, and then both will stop.

To injure another creates bondage and hides the truth. Negative virtues are not enough; we have to conquer Maya, and then she will follow us. We only deserve things when they cease to bind us. When the bondage ceases, really and truly, all things come to us. Only those who want nothing are masters of nature.

The animal man lives in the senses. If he does not get enough to eat, he is miserable; or if something happens to his body, he is miserable. In the senses both his misery and his happiness begin and end. As soon as this man progresses, as soon as his horizon of happiness increases, his horizon of unhappiness increases proportionately.

The man in the forest does not know what it is to be jealous, to be in the law courts, to pay taxes, to be blamed by society, to be ruled over day and night by the most tremendous tyranny that human diabolism ever invented, which pries into the secrets of every human heart. He does not know how man becomes a thousand times more diabolical than any other animal, with all his vain knowledge and with all his pride.

Thus it is that, as we emerge out of the senses, we develop higher powers of enjoyment, and at the same time we have to develop higher powers of suffering too. The nerves become finer and capable off more suffering. In every society, we often find that the ignorant, common man, when abused, does not feel much, but he feels a good thrashing.

But the gentleman cannot bear a single word of abuse; he has become so finely nerved. Misery has increased with his susceptibility to happiness. This does not go much to prove the evolutionist's case.

As we increase our power to be happy, we also increase our power to suffer, and sometimes I am inclined to think that if we increase our power to become happy in arithmetical progression, we shall increase, on the other hand, our power to become miserable in geometrical progression. We who are progressing know that the more we progress, the more avenues are opened to pain as well as to pleasure. And this is Maya.

Thus we find that Maya is not a theory for the explanation of the world; it is simply a statement of facts as they exist, that the very basis of our being is contradiction, that everywhere we have to move through this tremendous contradiction, that wherever there is good, there must also be evil, and wherever there is evil, there must be some good, wherever there is life, death must follow as its shadow, and everyone who smiles will have to weep, and vice versa.

Nor can this state of things be remedied. We may verily imagine that there will be a place where there will be only good and no evil, where we shall only smile and never weep. This is impossible in the very nature of things; for the conditions will remain the same. Wherever there is the power of producing a smile in us, there lurks the power of producing tears. Wherever there is the power of producing happiness, there lurks somewhere the power of making us miserable.

Cause and effect are all Maya, and we shall grow to understand that all we see is as disconnected as the child's fairy tales now seem to us. There is really no such thing as cause and effect and we shall come to know it.

Then if you can, lower your intellect to let any allegory pass through your mind without questioning about connection. Develop love of imagery and beautiful poetry and then enjoy all mythologies as poetry.

Come not to mythology with ideas of history and reasoning. Let it flow as a current through your mind, let it be whirled as a candle before your eyes, without asking who holds the candle, and you will get the circle; the residuum of truth will remain in your mind.

Consciousness is a bondage. The argument from design claims that intelligence precedes form; but if intelligence is the cause of anything, it itself is in its turn an effect. It is Maya. God creates us, and we create God, and this is Maya.

The circle is unbroken; mind creates body, and body creates mind; the egg brings the chicken, the chicken the egg; the tree the seed, the seed the tree. The world is neither entirely differentiated nor yet entirely homogeneous. Man is free and must rise above both sides. Both are right in their place; but to reach truth, "isness", we must transcend all that we now know of existence, will, consciousness, doing, going, knowing.

There is no real individuality of the Jiva (separate soul); eventually it, as a compound, will go to pieces. Only that which is beyond further analysis is "simple", and that alone is truth, freedom, immortality, bliss.

All struggles for the preservation of this illusive individuality are really vices. All struggles to lose this individuality are virtues. Everything in the universe is trying to break down this individuality, either consciously or unconsciously. All morality is based upon the destruction of separateness or false individuality, because that is the cause of all sin.

Morality exists first; later, religion codifies it. Customs come first, and then mythology follows to explain them. While things are happening, they come by a higher law than reasoning; that arises later in the attempt to understand them. Reasoning is not the motive power, it is "chewing the cud" afterwards. Reason is the historian of the actions of the human beings.

In this world of Maya one need not injure, but "spread the hood, without striking". That is enough.

Delusion creates delusion. Delusion creates itself and destroys itself, such is Maya. All knowledge (so-called), being based on Maya, is a vicious circle, and in time that very knowledge destroys itself. "Let go the rope", delusion cannot touch the Atman. When we lay hold of the rope — identify ourselves with Maya — she has power over us. Let go of it, be the Witness only, then you can admire the picture of the universe undisturbed.

Maya is not illusion as it is popularly interpreted. Maya is real, yet it is not real. It is real in that the Real is behind it and gives it its appearance of reality. That which is real in Maya is the Reality in and through Maya. Yet the Reality is never seen ; and hence that which is seen is unreal, and it has no real independent existence of itself, but is dependent upon the Real for its existence.

Maya then is a paradox—real, yet not real, an illusion, yet not an illusion. He who knows the Real sees in Maya not illusion, but reality. He who knows not the Real sees in Maya illusion and thinks it real.

What we call nature is not the substance, unchanging and indestructible. Nature is time, space and causation. Nature is name and form. Nature is Mâyâ. Maya means name and form, into which everything is cast. Maya is not real. We could not destroy it or change it if it were real. The substance is the noumenon, Maya is phenomena. There is the real "me" which nothing can destroy, and there is the phenomenal "me" which is continually changing and disappearing.

Advaita means non-duality; there are no two, but one. Yet we see that here is a proposition that the Absolute is manifesting Itself as many, through the veil of time, space, and causation. Therefore it seems that here are two, the Absolute and Mâyâ (the sum total of time, space, and causation).

It seems apparently very convincing that there are two. To this the Advaitist replies that it cannot be called two. To have two, we must have two absolute independent existences which cannot be caused.

In the first place time, space, and causation cannot be said to be independent existences. Time is entirely a dependent existence; it changes with every change of our mind. Sometimes in dream one imagines that one has lived several years, at other times several months were passed as one second. So, time is entirely dependent on our state of mind.

Secondly, the idea of time vanishes altogether, sometimes. So with space. We cannot know what space is. Yet it is there, indefinable, and cannot exist separate from anything else. So with causation.

The one peculiar attribute we find in time, space, and causation is that they cannot exist separate from other things. Try to think of space without colour, or limits, or any connection with the things around — just abstract space. You cannot; you have to think of it as the space between two limits or between three objects. It has to be connected with some object to have any existence.

So with time; you cannot have any idea of abstract time, but you have to take two events, one preceding and the other succeeding, and join the two events by the idea of succession. Time depends on two events, just as space has to be related to outside objects. And the idea of causation is inseparable from time and space.

This is the peculiar thing about them that they have no independent existence. They have not even the existence which the chair or the wall has. They are as shadows around everything which you cannot catch. They have no real existence; yet they are not non-existent, seeing that through them all things are manifesting as this universe.

Thus we see, first, that the combination of time, space, and causation has neither existence nor non-existence. Secondly, it sometimes vanishes. To give an illustration, there is a wave on the ocean. The wave is the same as the ocean certainly, and yet we know it is a wave, and as such different from the ocean.

What makes this difference? The name and the form, that is, the idea in the mind and the form. Now, can we think of a wave-form as something separate from the ocean? Certainly not. It is always associated with the ocean idea. If the wave subsides, the form vanishes in a moment, and yet the form was not a delusion. So long as the wave existed the form was there, and you were bound to see the form. This is Maya.

What you call matter, or spirit, or mind, or anything else you may like to call them, the fact remains the same: we cannot say that they are, we cannot say that they are not. We cannot say they are one, we cannot say they are many. This eternal play of light and darkness — indiscriminate, indistinguishable, inseparable — is always there.

A fact, yet at the same time not a fact; awake and at the same time asleep. This is a statement of facts, and this is what is called Maya. We are born in this Maya, we live in it, we think in it, we dream in it. We are philosophers in it, we are spiritual men in it, nay, we are devils in this Maya, and we are gods in this Maya.

Stretch your ideas as far as you can make them higher and higher, call them infinite or by any other name you please, even these ideas are within this Maya. It cannot be otherwise, and the whole of human knowledge is a generalization of this Maya trying to know it as it appears to be.

This is the work of Nâma-Rupa — name and form. Everything that has form, everything that calls up an idea in your mind, is within Maya; for everything that is bound by the laws of time, space, and causation is within Maya.

In the scriptures on Bhakti, five different paths of relationship are mentioned, by any of which one can attain to God; but another one can very well be added to them, viz. the path of meditation on the non-separateness, or oneness with God.

Thus the Bhakta can call the Advaitins Bhaktas as well, but of the non-differentiating type. As long as one is within the region of Mâya, so long the idea of duality will no doubt remain. Space-time-causation, or name-and-form, is what is called Maya. When one goes beyond this Maya, then only the Oneness is realised, and then man is neither a dualist nor an Advaitist — to him all is One.

There is one thing between the metaphysical and the moral aspect of Advaitism; it is the theory of Mâyâ. Everyone of these points in the Advaita system requires years to understand and months to explain.

Therefore you will excuse me if I only just touch them en passant. This theory of Maya has been the most difficult thing to understand in all ages. Let me tell you in a few words that it is surely no theory, it is the combination of the three ideas Desha-Kâla-Nimitta — space, time, and causation — and this time and space and cause have been further reduced into Nâma-Rupa. Suppose there is a wave in the ocean.

The wave is distinct from the ocean only in its form and name, and this form and this name cannot have any separate existence from the wave; they exist only with the wave. The wave may subside, but the same amount of water remains, even if the name and form that were on the wave vanish for ever.

So this Maya is what makes the difference between me and you, between all animals and man, between gods and men. In fact, it is this Maya that causes the Atman to be caught, as it were, in so many millions of beings, and these are distinguishable only through name and form. If you leave it alone, let name and form go, all this variety vanishes for ever, and you are what you really are. This is Maya.

We sometimes indicate a thing by describing its surroundings. When we say "Sachchidananda" (Existence-Knowledge-Bliss), we are merely indicating the shores of an indescribable Beyond. Not even can we say "is" about it, for that too is relative. Any imagination, any concept is in vain. Neti, neti ("Not this, not this") is all that can be said, for even to think is to limit and so to lose.

The senses cheat you day and night. Vedanta found that out ages ago; modern science is just discovering the same fact. A picture has only length and breadth, and the painter copies nature in her cheating by artificially giving the appearance of depth. No two people see the same world.

The highest knowledge will show you that there is no motion, no change in anything; that the very idea of it is all Maya. Study nature as a whole, that is, study motion. Mind and body are not our real self; both belong to nature, but eventually we can know the ding an sich. Then mind and body being transcended, all that they conceive goes. When you cease utterly to know and see the world, then you realise Atman. The superseding of relative knowledge is what we want. There is no infinite mind or infinite knowledge, because both mind and knowledge are limited.

We are now seeing through a veil; then we reach the "x", which is the Reality of all our knowing. If we look at a picture through a pin-hole in a cardboard, we get an utterly mistaken notion; yet what we see is really the picture. As we enlarge the hole, we get a clearer and clearer idea.

Out of the reality we manufacture the different views in conformity with our mistaken perceptions of name and form. When we throw away the cardboard, we see the same picture, but we see it as it is. We put in all the attributes, all the errors; the picture itself is unaltered thereby.

That is because Atman is the reality of all; all we see is Atman, but not as we see it, as name and form; they are all in our veil, in Maya.

They are like spots in the object-glass of a telescope, yet it is the light of the sun that shows us the spots; we could not even see the illusion save for the background of reality which is Brahman. Swami Vivekananda is just the speck on the object-glass; I am Atman, real, unchangeable, and that reality alone enables me to see Swami Vivekananda.

Atman is the essence of every hallucination; but the sun is never identified with the spots on the glass, it only shows them to us. Our actions, as they are evil or good, increase or decrease the "spots"; but they never affect the God within us. Perfectly cleanse the mind of spots and instantly we see, "I and my father are one".

We first perceive, then reason later. We must have this perception as a fact, and it is called religion, realisation. No matter if one never heard of creed or prophet or book. Let him get this realisation, and he needs no more. Cleanse the mind, this is all of religion; and until we ourselves clear off the spots, we cannot see the Reality as it is.

The baby sees no sun; he has not yet the measure of it in himself. Get rid of the defects within yourself, and you will not be able to see any without.

A baby sees robbery done, and it means nothing to him. Once you find the hidden object in a puzzle picture, you see it ever more; so when once you are free and stainless, you see only freedom and purity in the world around. That moment all the knots of the heart are cut asunder, all crooked places are made straight, and this world vanishes as a dream. And when we awake, we wonder how we ever came to dream such trash!

According to the Advaita philosophy, there is only one thing real in the universe, which it calls Brahman; everything else is unreal, manifested and manufactured out of Brahman by the power of Mâyâ. To reach back to that Brahman is our goal.

We are, each one of us, that Brahman, that Reality, plus this Maya. If we can get rid of this Maya or ignorance, then we become what we really are. According to this philosophy, each man consists of three parts — the body, the internal organ or the mind, and behind that, what is called the Âtman, the Self.

The body is the external coating and the mind is the internal coating of the Atman who is the real perceiver, the real enjoyer, the being in the body who is working the body by means of the internal organ or the mind.

"Om tat sat" is the only thing beyond Maya, but God exists eternally. As long as the Niagara Falls exist, the rainbow will exist; but the water continually flows away. The falls are the universe, and the rainbow is personal God; and both are eternal. While the universe exists, God must exist.

God creates the universe, and the universe creates God; and both are eternal. Maya is neither existence nor non-existence. Both the Niagara Falls and the rainbow are eternally changeable. . . . Brahman seen through Maya. Persians and Christians split Maya into two and call the good half "God" and the bad half the "devil". Vedanta takes Maya as a whole and recognises a unity beyond it — Brahman. . .

Control Your Thoughts

Always keep your mind joyful; if melancholy thoughts come, kick them out.

Thoughts can be guided and controlled. ... [The Yogis of India] practiced to see how far the thoughts can be guided and controlled. By dint of hard work, thoughts may be silenced altogether. If thoughts were [the real man], as soon as thought ceases, he ought to die.

Thought ceases in meditation; even the mind's elements are quite quiet. Blood circulation stops. His breath stops, but he is not dead. If thought were he, the whole thing ought to go, but they find it does not go. That is practical [proof]. They came to the conclusion that even mind and thought were not the real man. Then speculation showed that it could not be.

If I have to please the world, that will be injuring the world; the voice of the majority is wrong, seeing that they govern and make the sad state of the world. Every new thought must create opposition — in the civilised a polite sneer, in the vulgar savage howls and filthy scandals.

Language is not the result of convention; it is not that people ever agreed to represent certain ideas by certain words; there never was an idea without a corresponding word or a word without a corresponding idea; ideas and words are in their nature inseparable. The symbols to represent ideas may be sound symbols or colour symbols. Deaf and dumb people have to think with other than sound symbols. Every thought in the mind has a form as its counterpart. This is called in Sanskrit philosophy Nâma-Rupa — name and form.

Whatever you dream and think of, you create. If it is hell, you die and see hell. If it is evil and Satan, you get a Satan. If ghosts, you get ghosts. Whatever you think, that you become. If you have to think, think good thoughts, great thoughts.

This taking for granted that you are weak little worms! By declaring we are weak, we become weak, we do not become better. Suppose we put out the light, close the windows, and call the room dark. Think of the nonsense!

What good does it do me to say I am a sinner? If I am in the dark, let me light a lamp. The whole thing is gone. Yet how curious is the nature of men! Though always conscious that the universal mind is behind their life, they think more of Satan, of darkness and lies. You tell them the truth — they do not see it; they like darkness better.

Religion belongs to the supersensuous and not to the sense plane. It is beyond all reasoning and is not on the plane of intellect. It is a vision, an inspiration, a plunge into the unknown and unknowable, making the unknowable more than known for it can never be "known".

This search has been in the human mind, as I believe, from the very beginning of humanity. There cannot have been human reasoning and intellect in any period of the world's history without this struggle, this search beyond. In our little universe, this human mind, we see a thought arise. Whence it arises we do not know; and when it disappears, where it goes, we know not either.

Words are only a mode of mind acting on mind. Good and evil thoughts are each a potent power, and they fill the universe. As vibration continues so thought remains in the form of thought until translated into action.

For example, force is latent in the man's arm until he strikes a blow, when he translates it into activity. We are the heirs of good and evil thought. If we make ourselves pure and the instruments of good thoughts, these will enter us. The good soul will not be receptive to evil thoughts. Evil thoughts find the best field in evil people; they are like microbes which germinate and increase only when they find a suitable soil.

Mere thoughts are like little waveless; fresh impulses to vibration come to them simultaneously, until at last one great wave seems to stand up and swallow up the rest. These universal thought-waves seem to recur every five hundred years, when invariably the great wave typifies and swallows up the others.

It is this which constitutes a prophet. He focuses in his own mind the thought of the age in which he is living and gives it back to mankind in concrete form. Krishna, Buddha, Christ, Mohammed, and Luther may be instanced as the great waves that stood up above their fellows (with a probable lapse of five hundred years between them). Always the wave that is backed by the greatest purity and the noblest character is what breaks upon the world as a movement of social reform.

Once again in our day there is a vibration of the waves of thought and the central idea is that of the Immanent God, and this is everywhere cropping up in every form and every sect. In these waves, construction alternates with destruction; yet the construction always makes an end of the work of destruction.

Now, as a man dives deeper to reach his spiritual nature, he feels no longer bound by superstition. The majority of sects will be transient, and last only as bubbles because the leaders are not usually men of character. Perfect love, the heart never reacting, this is what builds character. There is no allegiance possible where there is no character in the leader, and perfect purity ensures the most lasting allegiance and confidence.

Take up an idea, devote yourself to it, struggle on in patience, and the sun will rise for you.

There is a great tendency in modern times to talk too much of work and decry thought. Doing is very good, but that comes from thinking. Little manifestations of energy through the muscles are called work.

But where there is no thought, there will be no work. Fill the brain, therefore, with high thoughts, highest ideals, place them day and night before you, and out of that will come great work. Talk not about impurity, but say that we are pure. We have hypnotised ourselves into this thought that we are little, that we are born, and that we are going to die, and into a constant state of fear.

Thinking beings must differ; difference is the first sign of thought. If I am a thoughtful man, certainly I ought to like to live amongst thoughtful persons where there are differences of opinion.

Thought is all important, for "what we think we become".

There was once a Sannyâsin, a holy man, who sat under a tree and taught the people. He drank milk, and ate only fruit, and made endless "Prânâyâmas", and felt himself to be very holy. In the same village lived an evil woman.

Every day the Sannyasin went and warned her that her wickedness would lead her to hell. The poor woman, unable to change her method of life which was her only means of livelihood, was still much moved by the terrible future depicted by the Sannyasin. She wept and prayed to the Lord, begging Him to forgive her because she could not help herself. By and by both the holy man and the evil woman died.

The angels came and bore her to heaven, while the demons claimed the soul of the Sannyasin. "Why is this!" he exclaimed, "have I not lived a most holy life, and preached holiness to everybody? Why should I be taken to hell while this wicked woman is taken to heaven?"

"Because," answered the demons, "while she was forced to commit unholy acts, her mind was always fixed on the Lord and she sought deliverance, which has now come to her. But you, on the contrary, while you performed only holy acts, had your mind always fixed on the wickedness of others. You saw only sin, and thought only of sin, so now you have to go to that place where only sin is."

The moral of the story is obvious: The outer life avails little. The heart must be pure and the pure heart sees only good, never evil. We should never try to be guardians of mankind, or to stand on a pedestal as saints reforming sinners. Let us rather purify ourselves, and the result must be that in so doing we shall help others.

Thought is the finest and highest action of Prana. Thought, again, as we see, is not all. There is also what we call instinct or unconscious thought, the lowest plane of action. If a mosquito stings us, our hand will strike it automatically, instinctively. This is one expression of thought.

All reflex actions of the body belong to this plane of thought. There is again the other plane of thought, the conscious. I reason, I judge, I think, I see the pros and cons of certain things, yet that is not all.

We know that reason is limited. Reason can go only to a certain extent, beyond that it cannot reach. The circle within which it runs is very very limited indeed. Yet at the same time, we find facts rush into this circle. Like the coming of comets certain things come into this circle; it is certain they come from outside the limit, although our reason cannot go beyond.

The causes of the phenomena intruding themselves in this small limit are outside of this limit. The mind can exist on a still higher plane, the superconscious. When the mind has attained to that state, which is called Samâdhi — perfect concentration, superconsciousness — it goes beyond the limits of reason, and comes face to face with facts which no instinct or reason can ever know. All manipulations of the subtle forces of the body, the different manifestations of Prana, if trained, give a push to the mind, help it to go up higher, and become superconscious, from where it acts.

We are what our thoughts have made us; so take care of what you think. Words are secondary. Thoughts live, they travel far. Each thought we think is tinged with our own character, so that for the pure and holy man, even his jests or abuse will have the twist of his own love and purity and do good.

Whatever you think, that you will be. If you think yourselves weak, weak you will be; if you think yourselves strong, strong you will be; if you think yourselves impure, impure you will be; if you think yourselves pure, pure you will be.

The Value of Constant Practice

Abhyasa is constant practice of any one of the Yogas.

The mind should always go towards God. No other things have any right to withhold it. It should continuously think of God, though this is a very hard task; yet it can be done by persistent practice. What we are now is the result of our past practice. Again, practice makes us what we shall be.

So practice the other way; one sort of turning round has brought us this way, turn the other way and get out of it as soon as you can. Thinking of the senses has brought us down here — to cry one moment, to rejoice the next, to be at the mercy of every breeze, slave to everything.

This is shameful, and yet we call ourselves spirits. Go the other way, think of God; let the mind not think of any physical or mental enjoyment, but of God alone. When it tries to think of anything else, give it a good blow, so that it may turn round and think of God.

As oil poured from one vessel to another falls in an unbroken line, as chimes coming from a distance fall upon the ear as one continuous sound, so should the mind flow towards God in one continuous stream. We should not only impose this practice on the mind, but the senses too should be employed. Instead of hearing foolish things, we must hear about God; instead of talking foolish words, we must talk of God. Instead of reading foolish books, we must read good ones which tell of God.

The greatest aid to this practice of keeping God in memory is, perhaps, music. The Lord says to Nârada, the great teacher of Bhakti, “I do not live in heaven, nor do I live in the heart of the Yogi, but where My devotees sing My praise, there am I”.

Music has such tremendous power over the human mind; it brings it to concentration in a moment. You will find the dull, ignorant, low, brute-like human beings, who never steady their mind for a moment at other times, when they hear attractive music, immediately become charmed and concentrated. Even the minds of animals, such as dogs, lions, cats, and serpents, become charmed with music.

The real work is in the practice. Are any practices necessary to realise this Oneness? Most decidedly. It is not that you become this Brahman. You are already that. It is not that you are going to become God or perfect; you are already perfect; and whenever you think you are not, it is a delusion.

This delusion which says that you are Mr. So-and-so or Mrs. So-and-so can be got rid of by another delusion, and that is practice. Fire will eat fire, and you can use one delusion to conquer another delusion. One cloud will come and brush away another cloud, and then both will go away.

What are these practices then? We must always bear in mind that we are not going to be free, but are free already. Every idea that we are bound is a delusion. Every idea that we are happy or unhappy is a tremendous delusion; and another delusion will come — that we have got to work and worship and struggle to be free — and this will chase out the first delusion, and then both will stop.

The Yogi must always practice. He should try to live alone; the companionship of different sorts of people distracts the mind; he should not speak much, because to speak distracts the mind; not work much, because too much work distracts the mind; the mind cannot be controlled after a whole day's hard work. One observing the above rules becomes a Yogi.

Such is the power of Yoga that even the least of it will bring a great amount of benefit. It will not hurt anyone, but will benefit everyone. First of all, it will tone down nervous excitement, bring calmness, enable us to see things more clearly. The temperament will be better, and the health will be better.

Sound health will be one of the first signs, and a beautiful voice. Defects in the voice will be changed. This will be among the first of the many effects that will come. Those who practise hard will get many other signs. Sometimes there will be sounds, as a peal of bells heard at a distance, commingling, and falling on the ear as one continuous sound. Sometimes things will be seen, little specks of light floating and becoming bigger and bigger; and when these things come, know that you are progressing fast.

The fox is considered very unholy by the Mohammedans and by the Hindus. Also, if a dog touches any bit of food, it has to be thrown out, it cannot be eaten by any man. In a certain Mohammedan house a fox entered and took a little bit of food from the table, ate it up, and fled.

The man was a poor man, and had prepared a very nice feast for himself, and that feast was made unholy, and he could not eat it. So he went to a Mulla, a priest, and said, "This has happened to me; a fox came and took a mouthful out of my meal. What can be done? I had prepared a feast and wanted so much to eat it, and now comes this fox and destroys the whole affair."

The Mulla thought for a minute and then found only one solution and said, "The only way for you is to get a dog and make him eat a bit out of the same plate, because dogs and foxes are eternally quarrelling. The food that was left by the fox will go into your stomach, and that left by the dog will go there too, and both will be purified."

We are very much in the same predicament. This is a hallucination that we are imperfect; and we take up another, that we have to practice to become perfect. Then one will chase the other, as we can use one thorn to extract another and then throw both away.

There are people for whom it is sufficient knowledge to hear, "Thou art That". With a flash this universe goes away and the real nature shines, but others have to struggle hard to get rid of this idea of bondage.

Through faithful practice, layer after layer of the mind opens before us, and each reveals new facts to us. We see as it were new worlds created before us, new powers are put into our hands, but we must not stop by the way or allow ourselves to be dazzled by these "beads of glass" when the mine of diamonds lies before us.

Whenever a prophet got into the superconscious state by heightening his emotional nature, he brought away from it not only some truths, but some fanaticism also, some superstition which injured the world as much as the greatness of the teaching helped. To get any reason out of the mass of incongruity we call human life, we have to transcend our reason, but we must do it scientifically, slowly, by regular practice, and we must cast off all superstition.

Says Patanjali, the father of Yoga, "When a man rejects all the superhuman powers, then he attains to the cloud of virtue." He sees God. He becomes God and helps others to become the same. This is all I have to preach. Doctrines have been expounded enough. There are books by the million. Oh, for an ounce of practice!

External practices have value only as helps to develop internal purity.

By practice men can bring even the heart under control, until it will just beat at will, slowly, or quickly, or almost stop. Nearly every part of the body can be brought under control.

My children, the secret of religion lies not in theories but in practice. o be good and to do good — that is the whole of religion. "Not he that crieth 'Lord', 'Lord', but he that doeth the will of the Father".

One ounce of practice is worth a thousand pounds of theory. One ounce of the practice of righteousness and of spiritual Self-realisation outweighs tons and tons of frothy talk and nonsensical sentiments.

In 1400 B.C. a great sage made an attempt to arrange, analyse, and generalise upon certain psychological facts. He was followed by many others who took up parts of what he had discovered and made a special study of them The Hindus alone of all ancient races took up the study of this branch of knowledge in right earnest.

I am teaching you now about it, but how many of you will practice it? How many days, how many months will it be before you give it up? You are impractical on this subject. In India, they will persevere for ages and ages. You will be astonished to hear that they have no churches, no Common Prayers, or anything of the kind; but they, every day, still practice the breathings and try to concentrate the mind; and that is the chief part of their devotion. These are the main points. Every Hindu must do these. It is the religion of the country.

Only, each one may have a special method — a special form of breathing, a special form of concentration, and what is one's special method, even one's wife need not know; the father need not know the son's. But they all have to do these.

And there is nothing occult about these things. The word "occult" has no bearing on them. Near the Gangâ thousands and thousands of people may be seen daily sitting on its banks breathing and concentrating with closed eyes.

There may be two reasons that make certain practices impracticable for the generality of mankind. One is, the teachers hold that the ordinary people are not fit for them. There may be some truth in this, but it is due more to pride.

The second is the fear of persecution. A man, for instance, would not like to practice breathing publicly in this country, because he would be thought so queer; it is not the fashion here. On the other hand, in India. if a man prayed, "Give us this day our daily bread", people would laugh at him. Nothing could be more foolish to the Hindu mind than to say, "Our Father which art in Heaven." The Hindu, when he worships, thinks that God is within himself.

Practice is absolutely necessary. You may sit down and listen to me by the hour every day, but if you do not practice, you will not get one step further. It all depends on practice.

We never understand these things until we experience them. We will have to see and feel them for ourselves. Simply listening to explanations and theories will not do. There are several obstructions to practice.

The first obstruction is an unhealthy body: if the body is not in a fit state, the practice will be obstructed. Therefore we have to keep the body in good health; we have to take care of what we eat and drink, and what we do. Always use a mental effort, what is usually called "Christian Science," to keep the body strong. That is all — nothing further of the body. We must not forget that health is only a means to an end. If health were the end, we would be like animals; animals rarely become unhealthy.

The second obstruction is doubt; we always feel doubtful about things we do not see. Man cannot live upon words, however he may try. So, doubt comes to us as to whether there is any truth in these things or not; even the best of us will doubt sometimes: With practice, within a few days, a little glimpse will come, enough to give one encouragement and hope.

As a certain commentator on Yoga philosophy says, "When one proof is obtained, however little that may be, it will give us faith in the whole teaching of Yoga."

For instance, after the first few months of practice, you will begin to find you can read another's thoughts; they will come to you in picture form. Perhaps you will hear something happening at a long distance, when you concentrate your mind with a wish to hear. These glimpses will come, by little bits at first, but enough to give you faith, and strength, and hope.

For instance, if you concentrate your thoughts on the tip of your nose, in a few days you will begin to smell most beautiful fragrance, which will be enough to show you that there are certain mental perceptions that can be made obvious without the contact of physical objects.

But we must always remember that these are only the means; the aim, the end, the goal, of all this training is liberation of the soul. Absolute control of nature, and nothing short of it, must be the goal. We must be the masters, and not the slaves of nature; neither body nor mind must be our master, nor must we forget that the body is mine, and not I the body's.

Man only remains hypnotised with the false idea of an ego. When this ghost is off from us, all dreams vanish, and then it is found that the one Self only exists from the highest Being to a blade of grass.

This will have to be known, to be realised. All practice or worship is only for taking off this veil. When that will go, you will find that the Sun of Absolute Knowledge is shining in Its own lustre. For the Atman only is self-luminous and has to be realised by Itself.

Only by practice and non-attachment can we conquer mind.

Perfection must come through the practice of holiness and love.

"We have to do something; let us do good." [But] who cares for good and evil? Play! God Almighty plays. That is all. You are the almighty God playing. If you want to play on the side and take the part of a beggar, you are not [to blame someone else for making that choice]. You enjoy being the beggar. You know your real nature [to be divine]. You are the king and play you are a beggar.

It is all fun. Know it and play. That is all there is to it. Then practice it. The whole universe is a vast play.

A child begins to play on the piano. At first she must pay attention to every key she is fingering, and as she goes on and on for months and years, the playing becomes almost involuntary, instinctive. What was first done with conscious will does not require later on an effort of the will. Almost all the actions which are now instinctive can be brought under the control of the will. Each muscle of the body can be brought under control. This is perfectly well known.

However sublime be the theories, however well-spun may be the philosophy — I do not call it religion so long as it is confined to books and dogmas. The eye is in the forehead and not in the back. Move onward and carry into practice that which you are very proud to call your religion, and God bless you!

Be Fearless

One part of the doctrine of Karma-Yoga is activity, the duty of the householder. There is a passage later on, where it says that "if the householder dies in battle, fighting for his country or his religion, he comes to the same goal as the Yogi by meditation," showing thereby that what is duty for one is not duty for another.

At the same time, it does not say that this duty is lowering and the other elevating. Each duty has its own place, and according to the circumstances in which we are placed, we must perform our duties.

One idea comes out of all this — the condemnation of all weakness. This is a particular idea in all our teachings which I like, either in philosophy, or in religion, or in work. If you read the Vedas, you will find this word always repeated — fearlessness — fear nothing. Fear is a sign of weakness. A man must go about his duties without taking notice of the sneers and the ridicule of the world.

We go through the world like a man pursued by a policeman and see the barest glimpses of the beauty of it. All this fear that pursues us comes from believing in matter. Matter gets its whole existence from the presence of mind behind it. What we see is God percolating through nature.

Those who are protected by the Lord must be above fear.

I don't want to work. I want to be quiet and rest. I know the time and the place; but the fate or Karma, I think, drives me on — work, work. We are like cattle driven to the slaughter-house — hastily nibbling a bite of grass on the roadside as they are driven along under the whip.

And all this is our work, our fear — fear, the beginning of misery, of disease, etc. By being nervous and fearful we injure others, by being so fearful to hurt we hurt more. By trying so much to avoid evil we fall into its jaws.

What a mass of namby-pamby nonsense we create round ourselves! It does us no good, it leads us on to the very thing we try to avoid — misery.

Oh, to become fearless, to be daring, to be careless of everything!

We are all born cowards. If we can save ourselves [we care about nothing else]. Inside is the tremendous fear, the tremendous motive, all the time. Our own selfishness makes us the most arrant cowards; our own selfishness is the great cause of fear and cowardice.

Fear never leaves those who earn their livelihoods by unethical means or who cause harm to others. Therefore, at this time when we face the great fear of death, desist from all such behaviour.

"In wealth is the fear of poverty, in knowledge the fear of ignorance, in beauty the fear of age, in fame the fear of backbiters, in success the fear of jealousy, even in body is the fear of death. Everything in this earth is fraught with fear. He alone is fearless who has given up everything" (Vairâgya-Shatakam, 31).

You believe in God. If you do, believe in the real God. "Thou art the man, thou the woman, thou the young man walking in the strength of youth, thou the old man tottering with his stick." (Shvetâshvatara, IV. 3.) Thou art weakness. Thou art fear. Thou art heaven, and Thou art hell. Thou art the serpent that would sting. Come thou as fear! Come thou as death! Come thou as misery!

All weakness, all bondage is imagination. Speak one word to it, it must vanish. Do not weaken! There is no other way out. Stand up and be strong! No fear. No superstition. Face the truth as it is! If death comes — that is the worst of our miseries — let it come! We are determined to die game. That is all the religion I know. I have not attained to it, but I am struggling to do it. I may not, but you may. Go on!

He who thinks himself free, free he becomes; he who thinks himself bound, bound he remains — this popular saying is true: 'As one thinks, so one becomes'." He alone who is always awake to the idea of freedom, becomes free; he who thinks he is bound, endures life after life in the state of bondage. It is a fact.

This truth holds good both in spiritual and temporal matters. Those who are always down-hearted and dispirited in this life can do no work; from life to life they come and go wailing and moaning. "The earth is enjoyed by heroes" — this is the unfailing truth.

Be a hero. Always say, "I have no fear." Tell this to everybody — "Have no fear".

Fear is death, fear is sin, fear is hell, fear is unrighteousness, fear is wrong life. All the negative thoughts and ideas that are in this world have proceeded from this evil spirit of fear. This fear alone has kept the sun, air and death in their respective places and functions, allowing none to escape from their bounds.

Therefore the Shruti says (Katha Upanishad, II. iii, 3) says:

"Through fear of this, fire burns, the sun heats; through fear Indra and Vâyu are carrying on their functions, and Death stalks upon this earth."

When the gods Indra, Chandra, Vayu, Varuna will attain to fearlessness, then will they be one with Brahman, and all this phantasm of the world will vanish. Therefore I say, "Be fearless, be fearless." Do not be afraid.

Fear never leaves those who earn their livelihoods by unethical means or who cause harm to others. Therefore, at this time when we face the great fear of death, desist from all such behaviour.

Generally speaking, human religion begins with fear. "The fear of the Lord is the beginning of wisdom." But later comes the higher idea. "Perfect love casteth out fear." Traces of fear will remain with us until we get knowledge, know what God is.

Christ, being man, had to see impurity and denounced it; but God, infinitely higher, does not see iniquity and cannot be angry. Denunciation is never the highest. David's hands were smeared with blood; he could not build the temple. (Bible, Samuel, Chap. XVII — end.)

A great source of misery is fear. Why does one man injure another? Because he fears he will not have enough enjoyment. One man fears that, perhaps, he will not have enough money, and that fear causes him to injure others and rob them.

How can there be fear if there is only one existence? If a thunderbolt falls on my head, it was I who was the thunderbolt, because I am the only existence. If a plague comes, it is I; if a tiger comes, it is I. If death comes, it is I. I am both death and life.

We see that fear comes with the idea that there are two in the universe. We have always heard it preached, "Love one another". What for? That doctrine was preached, but the explanation is here. Why should I love every one? Because they and I are one. Why should I love my brother? Because he and I are one.

There is this oneness; this solidarity of the whole universe. From the lowest worm that crawls under our feet to the highest beings that ever lived — all have various bodies, but are the one Soul. Through all mouths, you eat; through all hands, you work; through all eyes, you see. You enjoy health in millions of bodies, you are suffering from disease in millions of bodies.

When this idea comes, and we realise it, see it, feel it, then will misery cease, and fear with it. How can I die? There is nothing beyond me. Fear ceases, and then alone comes perfect happiness and perfect love.

In this world we work through fear of others, we talk through fear, we think through fear, alas! we are born in a land of enemies. Who is there who has been able to get rid of this feeling of fear, as if everyone is a spy set specially to watch him? And woe unto the man who pushes himself forward! Will it ever be a land of friends? Who knows?

Straying away from the true path of the Shastras, the country has been overwhelmed with usages and observances originating in particular localities, or popular opinion, or with the womenfolk! That's why I ask you to proceed along the path of the Shastras as in olden times.

Have faith within yourselves and thereby bring it back into the country. Plant in your heart the faith of Nachiketâ. Even go up to the world of Yama like him.

Yes, if to know the secrets of the Atman, to liberate your soul, to reach the true solution of the mystery of birth and death, you have to go to the very jaws of death and realise the truth thereby, well, go there with an undaunted heart. It is fear alone that is death. You have to go beyond all fear. So from this day be fearless.

Please do not panic due to unfounded fear. Depend upon God and calmly try to find the best means to solve the problem. Otherwise, join hands with those who are doing that very thing.

What is there to fear? The terror that has entered people's hearts due to the occurrence of the plague has no real ground. Through God's will, nothing of the terrible form that plague takes, as seen in other places, has occurred in Calcutta. The government authorities have also been particularly helpful to us. So what is there to fear?

Come, let us give up this false fear and, having faith in the infinite compassion of God, gird our loins and enter the field of action. Let us live pure and clean lives. Disease, fear of an epidemic, etc., will vanish into thin air by His grace.

The first thing to be got rid of by him who would be a Jnani is fear. Fear is one of our worst enemies.

This I have seen in life — he who is over-cautious about himself falls into dangers at every step; he who is afraid of losing honour and respect, gets only disgrace; he who is always afraid of loss always loses.

What fear! Whom to fear! Steel your hearts and set yourselves to work!

What fear is there? Always discriminate — your body, your house, these Jivas and the world are all absolutely unreal like a dream. Always think that this body is only an inert instrument. And the self – contained Purusha within is your real nature.

The mind has to be killed. When the mind dies, all limiting adjuncts vanish and you are established in Brahman.

Strength, strength is what the Upanishads speak to me from every page. This is the one great thing to remember, it has been the one great lesson I have been taught in my life; strength, it says, strength, O man, be not weak. Are there no human weaknesses? — says man. There are, say the Upanishads, but will more weakness heal them, would you try to wash dirt with dirt? Will sin cure sin, weakness cure weakness? Strength, O man, strength, say the Upanishads, stand up and be strong.

Ay, it is the only literature in the world where you find the word "Abhih", "fearless", used again and again; in no other scripture in the world is this adjective applied either to God or to man. Abhih, fearless!

Be not afraid, for all great power, throughout the history of humanity, has been with the people. From out of their ranks have come all the greatest geniuses of the world, and history can only repeat itself.

Be not afraid of anything. You will do marvellous work. The moment you fear, you are nobody. It is fear that is the great cause of misery in the world. It is fear that is the greatest of all superstitions. It is fear that is the cause of our woes, and it is fearlessness that brings heaven even in a moment.

Up, up, the long night is passing, the day is approaching, the wave has risen, nothing will be able to resist its tidal fury. The spirit, my boys, the spirit; the love, my children, the love; the faith, the belief; and fear not! The greatest sin is fear.

Therefore, say the Vedas, "Arise, awake, and stop not till the goal is reached."

Infinite Patience, Infinite Perseverance

Are great things ever done smoothly? Time, patience, and indomitable will must show.

Every work has got to pass through hundreds of difficulties before succeeding. Those that persevere will see the light, sooner or later.

"Fortune favours the brave and energetic." Don't look back — forward, infinite energy, infinite enthusiasm, infinite daring, and infinite patience — then alone can great deeds be accomplished. We must set the whole world afire.

Have fire and spread all over. Work, work. Be the servant while leading, be unselfish, and never listen to one friend in private accusing another. Have infinite patience, and success is yours.

Have patience and be faithful unto death. Do not fight among yourselves. Be perfectly pure in money dealings… We will do great things yet… So long as you have faith and honesty and devotion, everything will prosper.

Shyness won't do any more.... He who has infinite patience and infinite energy at his back, will alone succeed.

Infinite patience, infinite purity, and infinite perseverance are the secret of success in a good cause.

The more heart you will be able to manifest, the greater will be the victory you achieve. It is only a few that understand the language of the brain, but everyone from the Creator down to a clump of grass, understands the language that comes from the heart.

But then, in our country, it is a case of rousing men that are, as it were, dead. It will take time, but if you have infinite patience and perseverance, success is bound to come. No mistake in that.

Know full well that patience is the best means of succeeds.

Know it for certain that without steady devotion for the Guru and unflinching patience and perseverance, nothing is to be achieved.

Love conquers in the long run. It won't do to become impatient — wait, wait — patience is bound to give success.

Can anything be done unless everybody exerts himself to his utmost? " " etc.— "It is the man of action, the lion-heart, that the Goddess of Wealth resorts to." No need for looking behind. FORWARD! We want infinite energy, infinite zeal, infinite courage, and infinite patience, then only will great things achieved.

Nothing else is necessary but these — love, sincerity, and patience.

Nothing shall be done in haste. Purity, patience, and perseverance are the three essentials to success and, above all, love. All time is yours, there is no indecent haste. Everything will come right if you are pure and sincere.

Persevere on, my brave lads, We have only just begun. Never despond! Never say enough!

Purity, perseverance, and energy— these three I want.

Purity, patience and perseverance overcome all obstacles. All great things must of necessity be slow.

The fruit falls from the tree when it gets ripe. So wait for the time to come. Do not hurry. Moreover, no one has the right to make others miserable by his foolish acts. Wait, have patience, everything will come right in time.

Those who really want to be Yogis must give up, once for all, this nibbling at things. Take up one idea. Make that one idea your life — think of it, dream of it, live on that idea. Let the brain, muscles, nerves, every part of your body, be full of that idea, and just leave every other idea alone.

This is the way to success, and this is the way great spiritual giants are produced. Others are mere talking machines. If we really want to be blessed, and make others blessed, we must go deeper.

The first step is not to disturb the mind, not to associate with persons whose ideas are disturbing. All of you know that certain persons, certain places, certain foods, repel you. Avoid them; and those who want to go to the highest, must avoid all company, good or bad.

Practise hard; whether you live or die does not matter. You have to plunge in and work, without thinking of the result. If you are brave enough, in six months you will be a perfect Yogi.

But those who take up just a bit of it and a little of everything else make no progress. It is of no use simply to take a course of lessons. To those who are full of Tamas, ignorant and dull — those whose minds never get fixed on any idea, who only crave for something to amuse them — religion and philosophy are simply objects of entertainment. These are the unpersevering. They hear a talk, think it very nice, and then go home and forget all about it.

To succeed, you must have tremendous perseverance, tremendous will. 'I will drink the ocean', says the persevering soul, 'at my will mountains will crumble up.' Have that sort of energy, that sort of will, work hard, and you will reach the goal.

Wait, my child, wait and work on. Patience, patience.

Rejoice that you have done so much. When you feel gloomy, think what has been done within the last year. How, rising from nothing, we have the eyes of the world fixed upon us now. Not only India, but the world outside, is expecting great things of us.

There was a great god-sage called Narada. Just as there are sages among mankind, great Yogis, so there are great Yogis among the gods. Narada was a good Yogi, and very great. He travelled everywhere.

One day he was passing through a forest, and saw a man who had been meditating until the white ants had built a huge mound round his body — so long had he been sitting in that position. He said to Narada, "Where are you going?"

Narada replied, "I am going to heaven."

"Then ask God when He will be merciful to me; when I shall attain freedom."

Further on Narada saw another man. He was jumping about, singing, dancing, and said, "Oh, Narada, where are you going?" His voice and his gestures were wild.

Narada said, "I am going to heaven."

"Then, ask when I shall be free."

Narada went on. In the course of time he came again by the same road, and there was the man who had been meditating with the ant-hill round him. He said, "Oh, Narada, did you ask the Lord about me?"

"Oh, yes."

"What did He say?"

"The Lord told me that you would attain freedom in four more births."

Then the man began to weep and wail, and said, "I have meditated until an ant-hill has grown around me, and I have four more births yet!"

Narada went to the other man. "Did you ask my question?"

"Oh, yes. Do you see this tamarind tree? I have to tell you that as many leaves as there are on that tree, so many times, you shall be born, and then you shall attain freedom."

The man began to dance for joy, and said, "I shall have freedom after such a short time!"

A voice came, "My child, you will have freedom this minute."

That was the reward for his perseverance. He was ready to work through all those births, nothing discouraged him. But the first man felt that even four more births were too long. Only perseverance, like that of the man who was willing to wait aeons brings about the highest result.

The most horrible thing about competition is that one may conquer the environments, but that where one may conquer, thousands are crowded out. So it is evil at best. That cannot be good which helps only one and hinders the majority. Patanjali says that these struggles remain only through our ignorance, and are not necessary, and are not part of the evolution of man. It is just our impatience which creates them.

We have not the patience to go and work our way out. For instance, there is a fire in a theatre, and only a few escape. The rest in trying to rush out crush one another down. That crush was not necessary for the salvation of the building nor of the two or three who escaped. If all had gone out slowly, not one would have been hurt.

That is the case in life. The doors are open for us, and we can all get out without the competition and struggle; and yet we struggle. The struggle we create through our own ignorance, through impatience; we are in too great a hurry. The highest manifestation of strength is to keep ourselves calm and on our own feet.

A Life of Sacrifice

In the animal kingdom we really see such laws as struggle for existence, survival of the fittest, etc., evidently at work. Therefore Darwin's theory seems true to a certain extent. But in the human kingdom, where there is the manifestation of rationality, we find just the reverse of those laws.

For instance, in those whom we consider really great men or ideal characters, we scarcely observe any external struggle. In the animal kingdom instinct prevails; but the more a man advances, the more he manifests rationality.

For this reason, progress in the rational human kingdom cannot be achieved, like that in the animal kingdom, by the destruction of others! The highest evolution of man is effected through sacrifice alone. A man is great among his fellows in proportion as he can sacrifice for the sake of others, while in the lower strata of the animal kingdom, that animal is the strongest which can kill the greatest number of animals.

Hence the struggle theory is not equally applicable to both kingdoms. Man's struggle is in the mental sphere. A man is greater in proportion as he can control his mind. When the mind's activities are perfectly at rest, the Atman manifests Itself.

The struggle which we observe in the animal kingdom for the preservation of the gross body obtains in the human plane of existence for gaining mastery over the mind or for attaining the state of balance. Like a living tree and its reflection in the water of a tank, we find opposite kinds of struggle in the animal and human kingdoms.

Do all as a sacrifice or offering to the Lord. Be in the world, but not of it, like the lotus leaf whose roots are in the mud but which remains always pure. Let your love go to all, whatever they do to you.

A blind man cannot see colour, so how can we see evil unless it is in us? We compare what we see outside with what we find in ourselves and pronounce judgment accordingly. Do not want this world, because what you desire you get.

Seek the Lord and the Lord only. The more power there is, the more bondage, the more fear. How much more afraid and miserable are we than the ant! Get out of it all and come to the Lord. Seek the science of the maker and not that of the made.

Great things can be done by great sacrifices only. No selfishness, no name, no fame, yours or mine, nor my Master's even! Work, work the idea, the plan, my boys, my brave, noble, good souls — to the wheel, to the wheel put your shoulders!

Stop not to look back for name, or fame, or any such nonsense. Throw self overboard and work. Remember, "The grass when made into a rope by being joined together can even chain a mad elephant."

The Lord's blessings on you all! His power be in you all— as I believe it is already . "Wake up, stop not until the goal is reached", say the Vedas.

Where is that martial spirit which, at the very outset, requires one to know how to serve and obey and to practise self-restraint! The martial spirit is not self – assertion but self – sacrifice. One must be ready to advance and lay down one's life at the word of command, before he can command the hearts and lives of others. One must sacrifice himself first.

I know, and know for sure, that great things are done only by great sacrifices. I know for certain that India requires the sacrifice of her highest and best.

Throughout the history of the world you find great men make great sacrifices and the mass of mankind enjoy the benefit. If you want to give up everything for your own salvation, it is nothing. Do you want to forgo even your own salvation for the good of the world? You are God, think of that.

I want a band of young Bengal — who alone are the hope of this country. My hope of the future lies in the youths of character — intelligent, renouncing all for the service of others, and obedient — who can sacrifice their lives in working out my ideas and thereby do good to themselves and the country at large.

Otherwise, boys of the common run are coming in groups and will come. Dullness is written on their faces — their hearts are devoid of energy, their bodies feeble and unfit for work, and minds devoid of courage. What work will be done by these? If I get ten or twelve boys with the faith of Nachiketâ, I can turn the thoughts and pursuits of this country in a new channel.

First, we have to understand the ideal, and then the methods by which we can make it practical. Those of you who are Sannyasins must try to do good to others, for Sannyasa means that.

There is no time to deliver a long discourse on "Renunciation", but I shall very briefly characterise it as "the love of death ". Worldly people love life. The Sannyasin is to love death.

Are we to commit suicide then? Far from it. For suicides are not lovers of death, as it is often seen that when a man trying to commit suicide fails, he never attempts it for a second time.

What is the love of death then? We must die, that is certain; let us die then for a good cause. Let all our actions — eating, drinking, and everything that we do — tend towards the sacrifice of our self.

You nourish your body by eating. What good is there in doing that if you do not hold it as a sacrifice to the well-being of others? You nourish your minds by reading books. There is no good in doing that unless you hold it also as a sacrifice to the whole world.

For the whole world is one; you are rated a very insignificant part of it, and therefore it is right for you that you should serve your millions of brothers rather than aggrandise this little self.

Thus you must die a gradual death. In such a death is heaven, all good is stored therein — and in its opposite is all that is diabolical and evil.

Then as to the methods of carrying the ideals into practical life. First, we have to understand that we must not have any impossible ideal. An ideal which is too high makes a nation weak and degraded. This happened after the Buddhistic and the Jain reforms.

On the other hand, too much practicality is also wrong. If you have not even a little imagination, if you have no ideal let guide you, you are simply a brute. So we must not lower our ideal, neither are we to lose sight of practicality. We must avoid the two extremes.

Let us be at peace, perfect peace, with ourselves, and give up our whole body and mind and everything as an eternal sacrifice unto the Lord. Instead of the sacrifice of pouring oblations into the fire, perform this one great sacrifice day and night — the sacrifice of your little self.

"In search of wealth in this world, Thou art the only wealth I have found; I sacrifice myself unto Thee. In search of some one to be loved, Thou art the only one beloved I have found; I sacrifice myself unto Thee."

Let us repeat this day and night, and say, "Nothing for me; no matter whether the thing is good, bad, or indifferent; I do not care for it; I sacrifice all unto Thee."

Day and night let us renounce our seeming self until it becomes a habit with us to do so, until it gets into the blood, the nerves, and the brain, and the whole body is every moment obedient to this idea of self-renunciation. Go then into the midst of the battlefield, with the roaring cannon and the din of war, and you will find yourself to be free and at peace.

No great thing can be done without sacrifice. Who on seeing the tiny sprout of the banyan can imagine that in course of time it will develop into a gigantic banyan tree?The heart must be plucked out and the bleeding heart placed upon the altar.

Then great things are done. Is there any other way? None have found it. I appeal to each one of you, to those who have accomplished any great thing. Oh, how much it has cost! What agony! What torture! What terrible suffering is behind every deed of success in every life! You know that, all of you.

Nothing is gained except by sacrifice. he holiest function of our human consciousness, the noblest, do not make it unclean! Do not degrade it to the level of the brutes.... Make yourselves decent men! ... Be chaste and pure! ... There is no other way. Did Christ find any other way? ... If you can conserve and use the energy properly, it leads you to God. Inverted, it is hell itself

One idea that I see clear as daylight is that misery is caused by ignorance and nothing else. Who will give the world light? Sacrifice in the past has been the Law, it will be, alas, for ages to come. The earth's bravest and best will have to sacrifice themselves for the good of many, for the welfare of all. Buddhas by the hundred are necessary with eternal love and pity.

Religions of the world have become lifeless mockeries. What the world wants is character. The world is in need of those whose life is one burning love, selfless. That love will make every word tell like thunderbolt.

Sacrifice of everything for the good of others is real Sannyasa. They have never enjoyed any good thing in life. See how simple they are. Can you mitigate their misery a little? Otherwise, of what good is the wearing of the Gerua robe?

No great work can be done without sacrifice. The Purusha Himself sacrificed Himself to create this world. Lay down your comforts, your pleasures, your names, fame or position, nay even your lives, and make a bridge of human chains over which millions will cross this ocean of life.

Bring all the forces of good together. Do not care under what banner you march. Do not care what be your colour — green, blue, or red — but mix up all the colours and produce that intense glow of white, the colour of love. Ours is to work. The results will take care of themselves.

If any social institution stands in your way of becoming God, it will give way before the power of Spirit. I do not see into the future; nor do I care to see. But one vision I see dear as life before me: that the ancient Mother has awakened once more, sitting on Her throne rejuvenated, more glorious than ever. Proclaim Her to all the world with the voice of peace and benediction.

Sacrifice on God's altar earth's purest and best. He who struggles is better than he who never attempts. Even to look on one who has given up has a purifying effect. Stand up for God; let the world go. Have no compromise.

Give up the world, then alone you are loosened from the body. When it dies, you are âzâd , free. Be free. Death alone can never free us. Freedom must be attained by our own efforts during life; then, when the body falls, there will be no rebirth for the free.

The two great watchwords of every great religion are renunciation and self – sacrifice. We all want the truth, and we know that it must come, whether we want it or not. In a way we are all striving for that good. And what prevents our reaching it? It is ourselves. Your ancestors used to call it the devil; but it is our own false self.

We live in slavery, and we would die if we were out of it. We are like the man who lived in total darkness for ninety years and when taken out into the warm sunshine of nature, prayed to be taken back to his dungeon. You would not leave this old life to go into a newer and greater freedom which opens out.

Sacrifice your life for the good of others and go round to the doors of people carrying this message of fearlessness — arise, awake, and stop not till the goal is reached.

"सन्निमित्ते वरं त्यागो विनाशे नियते सति—When death is certain, it is best to sacrifice oneself for a good cause."

We must plunge heart and soul and body into the work. Until we be ready to sacrifice everything else to one Idea and to one alone, we never, never will see the light. Those that want to help mankind must take their own pleasure and pain, name and fame, and all sorts of interests, and make a bundle of them and throw them into the sea, and then come to the Lord.

This is what all the Masters said and did. Was it ever in the history of the world that any great work was done by the rich? It is the heart and the brain that do it ever and ever and not the purse.

My idea and all my life with it — and to God for help; to none else! This is the only secret of success.

The ideal law may be that no man should covet the belongings of others, but the actual law is that a very large number do. Thus the word law used in regard to laws of nature has a very different interpretation when applied to ethics and human actions generally.

Analysing the ethical laws of the world and comparing them with the actual state of things, two laws stand out supreme. The one, that of repelling everything from us—separating ourselves from everyone—which leads to self-aggrandisement even at the cost of everyone else's happiness.

The other, that of self-sacrifice—of taking no thought of ourselves—only of others. Both spring from the search for happiness—one, of finding happiness in injuring others and the ability of feeling that happiness only in our own senses. The other, of finding happiness in doing good to others —the ability of feeling happy, as it were, through the senses of others.

The great and good of the world are those who have the latter power predominating. Yet both these are working side by side conjointly; in almost everyone they are found in mixture, one or the other predominating. The thief steals, perhaps, for someone he loves.

When you have men who are ready to sacrifice their everything for their country, sincere to the backbone — when such men arise, India will become great in every respect. It is the men that make the country!

What is there in the country? If you catch the social morality and the political morality of the Japanese, you will be as great as they are. The Japanese are ready to sacrifice everything for their country, and they have become a great people. But you are not; you cannot be, you sacrifice everything only for your own families and possessions.

The Karma-Yogi wants everyone to be saved before himself. His only salvation is to help others to salvation. "To serve Krishna's servants is the highest worship." One great saint prayed, "Let me go to hell with the sins of the whole world, but let the world be saved." True worship leads to intense self – sacrifice.

What good is it carrying along a load of bones and flesh! Initiated into the Mantra of extreme self-sacrifice for the sake of God, go, lay down for others this body of flesh and bones like the Muni Dadhichi! Those alone, say the Shastras, are the real Gurus, who have studied the Vedas and the Vedanta, who are knowers of the Brahman, who are able to lead others beyond to fearlessness; when such are at hand, get yourself initiated, "no speculation in such a case". Do you know what has become of this principle now? — "like the blind leading the blind"!

Love must conquer hatred, hatred cannot conquer itself. Materialism and all its miseries can never be conquered by materialism. Armies when they attempt to conquer armies only multiply and make brutes of humanity. Spirituality must conquer the West.

Where are the men ready to go out to every country in the world with the messages of the great sages of India? Where are the men who are ready to sacrifice everything, so that this message shall reach every corner of the world? Such heroic spurs are wanted to help the spread of truth.

Such heroic workers are wanted to go abroad and help to disseminate the great truths of the Vedanta. The world wants it; without it the world will be destroyed. The whole of the Western world is on a volcano which may burst tomorrow, go to pieces tomorrow. They have searched every corner of the world and have found no respite. They have drunk deep of the cup of pleasure and found it vanity. Now is the time to work so that India's spiritual ideas may penetrate deep into the West.

Therefore young men of Madras, I specially ask you to remember this. We must go out, we must conquer the world through our spirituality and philosophy. There is no other alternative, we must do it or die. The only condition of national life, of awakened and vigorous national life, is the conquest of the world by Indian thought.

As by continuing our religious practices we gradually develop a certain determined tendency for it, so by performing disinterested work over and over again, even unwillingly, we gradually find the will merging itself in it. The inclination to work for others develops in this way, do you see? Just do some such work even though unwillingly, and then see if the actual fruit of Tapasya is realised within or not. As the outcome of work for the sake of others, the angularities of the mind get smoothed down, and men are gradually prepared for sincere self-sacrifice for the good of others.

As the outcome of work for the sake of others, the angularities of the mind get smoothed down, and men are gradually prepared for sincere self – sacrifice for the good of others.

We should feel the Eternal Unity so much, that we should weep for all sinners, knowing that it is we who are sinning. The eternal law is self – sacrifice, not self – assertion. What self to assert when all is one? There are no "rights", all is love.

The great truths that Jesus taught have never been lived. Let us try his method and see if the world will not be saved. The contrary method has nearly destroyed it. Selflessness only, not selfishness, can solve the question.

The idea of "right" is a limitation; there is really no "mine" and "thine", for I am thou and thou art I. We have "responsibility", not "rights".

We should say, "I am the universe", not "I am John" or "I am Mary". These limitations are all delusions and are what holds us in bondage, for as soon as I think, "I am John", I want exclusive posses sion of certain things and begin to say "me and mine", and continually make new distinctions in so doing.

So our bondage goes on increasing with every fresh distinction, and we get further and further away from the central Unity, the undivided Infinite. There is only one Individual, and each of us is That.

Oneness alone is love and fearlessness; separation leads us to hatred and fear. Oneness fulfils the law. Here, on earth, we strive to enclose little spaces and exclude outsiders, but we cannot do that in the sky, though that is what sectarian religion tries to do when it says, "Only this way leads to salvation, all others are wrong".

Our aim should be to wipe out these little enclosures to widen the boundaries until they are lost sight of, and to realise that all religions lead to God. This little puny self must be sacrificed. This is the truth symbolised by baptism into a new life, the death of the old man, the birth of the new — the perishing of the false self, the realisation of the Atman, the one Self of the universe.

It is more blessed, in my opinion, even to go wrong, impelled by one's free will and intelligence than to be good as an automaton. Again, can that be called society which is formed by an aggregate of men who are like lumps of clay, like lifeless machines, like heaped up pebbles?

How can such society fare well? Were good possible, then instead of being slaves for hundreds of years, we would have been the greatest nation on earth, and this soil of India, instead of being a mine of stupidity, would have been the eternal fountain-head of learning. Is not self-sacrifice, then, a virtue? Is it not the most virtuous deed to sacrifice the happiness of one, the welfare of one, for the sake of the many?

It is all a degeneration which has its root in selfishness. That in boarding a steamer one follows the vulgar maxim, "Uncle, save thy own precious skin", and in music and moments of recreation everyone tries to make a display of himself, is a typical picture of our mental state. Only a little training in self – sacrifice would take it away. It is the fault of the parents who do not teach their children good manners. Self – sacrifice, indeed, is the basis of all civilization.

Exactly, but as the Bengali adage goes, "Can beauty be manufactured by rubbing and scrubbing? Can love be generated by effort and compulsion?" What glory is there in the renunciation of an eternal beggar? What virtue is there in the sense- control of one devoid of sense-power?

What again is the self-sacrifice of one devoid of idea, devoid of heart, devoid of high ambition, and devoid of the conception of what constitutes society? What expression of devotedness to a husband is there by forcing a widow to commit Sati? Why make people do virtuous deeds by teaching superstitions?

I say, liberate, undo the shackles of people as much as you can. Can dirt be washed by dirt? Can bondage be removed by bondage? Where is the instance? When you would be able to sacrifice all desire for happiness for the sake of society, then you would be the Buddha, then you would be free: that is far off.

Again, do you think the way to do it lies through oppression? "Oh, what examples or self-denial are our widows! Oh, how sweet is child-marriage! Is another such custom possible! Can there be anything but love between husband and wife in such a marriage!" such is the whine going round nowadays.

But as to the men, the masters of the situation, there is no need of self-denial for them! Is there a virtue higher than serving others? But the same does not apply to Brâhmins — you others do it!

The truth is that in this country parents and relatives can ruthlessly sacrifice the best interests of their children and others for their own selfish ends to save themselves by compromise to society; and the teaching of generations rendering the mind callous has made it perfectly easy. He, the brave alone, can deny self. The coward, afraid of the lash, with one hand wipes his eyes and gives with the other.

Of what avail are such gifts? It is a far cry to love universal. The young plant should be hedged in and taken care of. One can hope gradually to attain to universal love if one can learn to love one object unselfishly. If devotion to one particular Ishta-Deva is attained, devotion to the universal Virat is gradually possible.

Therefore, when one has been able to deny self for an individual, one should talk of self-sacrifice for the sake of society, not before. It is action with desire that leads to action without desire. Is the renunciation of desire possible if desire did not exist in the beginning? And what could it mean? Can light have any meaning if there is no darkness?

Worship with desire, with attachment, comes first. Commence with the worship of the little, then the greater will come of itself.

Purification through Self-Denial

You will find various classes of men in this world. There are the God-men, whose self-abnegation is complete, and who do only good to others even at the sacrifice of their own lives. These are the highest of men. If there are a hundred of such in any country, that country need never despair.

But they are unfortunately too few. Then there are the good men who do good to others so long as it does not injure themselves. And there is a third class who, to do good to themselves, injure others.

It is said by a Sanskrit poet that there is a fourth unnamable class of people who injure others merely for injury's sake. Just as there are at one pole of existence the highest good men, who do good for the sake of doing good, so, at the other pole, there are others who injure others just for the sake of the injury. They do not gain anything thereby, but it is their nature to do evil.

Here are two Sanskrit words. The one is Pravritti, which means revolving towards, and the other is Nivritti, which means revolving away. The "revolving towards" is what we call the world, the "I and mine"; it includes all those things which are always enriching that "me" by wealth and money and power, and name and fame, and which are of a grasping nature, always tending to accumulate everything in one centre, that centre being "myself".

That is the Pravritti, the natural tendency of every human being; taking everything from everywhere and heaping it around one centre, that centre being man's own sweet self. When this tendency begins to break, when it is Nivritti or "going away from," then begin morality and religion. Both Pravritti and Nivritti are of the nature of work: the former is evil work, and the latter is good work.

This Nivritti is the fundamental basis of all morality and all religion, and the very perfection of it is entire self-abnegation, readiness to sacrifice mind and body and everything for another being. When a man has reached that state, he has attained to the perfection of Karma-Yoga.

It is not at all any question of creed, or doctrine — even men who are very much opposed to all religious ideas, when they see one of these acts of complete self-sacrifice, feel that they must revere it.

Have you not seen even a most bigoted Christian, when he reads Edwin Arnold's Light of Asia, stand in reverence of Buddha, who Preached no God, preached nothing but self-sacrifice?

The only thing is that the bigot does not know that his own end and aim in life is exactly the same as that of those from whom he differs. The worshipper, by keeping constantly before him the idea of God and a surrounding of good, comes to the same point at last and says, "Thy will be done," and keeps nothing to himself. That is self-abnegation.

The philosopher, with his knowledge, sees that the seeming self is a delusion and easily gives it up. It is self-abnegation. So Karma, Bhakti, and Jnana all meet here; and this is what was meant by all the great preachers of ancient times, when they taught that God is not the world.

There is one thing which is the world and another which is God; and this distinction is very true. What they mean by world is selfishness. Unselfishness is God. One may live on a throne, in a golden palace, and be perfectly unselfish; and then he is in God. Another may live in a hut and wear rags, and have nothing in the world; yet, if he is selfish, he is intensely merged in the world.

Every act of charity, every thought of sympathy, every action of help, every good deed, is taking so much of self-importance away from our little selves and making us think of ourselves as the lowest and the least, and, therefore, it is all good. Here we find that Jnâna, Bhakti, and Karma — all come to one point.

The highest ideal is eternal and entire self-abnegation, where there is no "I," but all is "Thou"; and whether he is conscious or unconscious of it, Karma-Yoga leads man to that end. A religious preacher may become horrified at the idea of an Impersonal God; he may insist on a Personal God and wish to keep up his own identity and individuality, whatever he may mean by that.

But his ideas of ethics, if they are really good, cannot but be based on the highest self-abnegation. It is the basis of all morality; you may extend it to men, or animals, or angels, it is the one basic idea, the one fundamental principle running through all ethical systems.

The more a man throws himself away, the more God comes in, hence self abnegation, which is the secret of all religion and morality. Too many people bring down their ideals. They want a comfortable religion, but there is none such. It is all self-surrender and upward striving.

What is perfect self-abnegation? It means the abnegation of this apparent self, the abnegation of all selfishness. This idea of "me and mine" — Ahamkâra and Mamatâ — is the result of past Superstition, and the more this present self passes away, the more the real Self becomes manifest.

This is true self-abnegation, the centre, the basis, the gist of all moral teaching; and whether man knows it or not the whole world is slowly going towards it, practicing it more or less. Only, the vast majority of mankind are doing it unconsciously. Let them do it consciously. Let then make the sacrifice, knowing that this "me and mine" is not the real Self, but only a limitation.

But one glimpse Of that infinite reality which is behind — but one spark of that infinite fire that is the All — represents the present man; the Infinite is his true nature.

If we are genuine Karma-Yogis and wish to train ourselves to that attainment of this state, wherever we may begin we are sure to end in perfect self-abnegation; and as soon as this seeming self has gone, the whole world, which at first appears to us to be filled with evil, will appear to be heaven itself and full of blessedness. Its very atmosphere will be blessed; every human face there will be god. Such is the end and aim of Karma-Yoga, and such is its perfection in practical life.

The mission of the Institute of Thought and Philosophy is to preserve and propagate the teachings of Swami Vivekananda. This great Indian spiritual leader is known for introducing the West to Hinduism. Drawing from his vast literary legacy, we provide valuable insights and practical guidance for modern living.

Have any query or feedback? Please reach out to us at ITPPress123@gmail.com